PORTRAIT OF A SCANDAL

Shoshanna's Story

Journey to Vaja

Robert Weaver: Godfather of Canadian Literature

Storied Streets: Montreal in the Literary Imagination

Putting Down Roots

The Writers of Montreal

Portrait of a Scandal

~

The Abortion Trial of
Robert Notman

ELAINE KALMAN NAVES

Véhicule Press

Published with the generous assistance of the Canada Council for the Arts, the Canada Book Fund of the Department of Canadian Heritage, and the Société de développement des entreprises culturelles du Québec (SODEC).

Cover design: David Drummond
Typeset in Minion by Simon Garamond
Printed by Marquis Printing Inc.

LIBRARY AND ARCHIVES CANADA CATALOGUING IN PUBLICATION

Naves, Elaine Kalman, author
Portrait of a scandal : the abortion trial of Robert Notman /
Elaine Kalman Naves.

Includes bibliographical references.
ISBN 978-1-55065-357-1 (pbk.)

1. Notman, Robert. 2. Notman, Robert–Trials, litigation, etc.
3. Scots–Québec (Province)–Montréal–Biography. 4. Trials (Abortion)–
Québec (Province)–Montréal–History–19th century.
5. Montréal (Québec)–Biography. I. Title.

Published by Véhicule Press, Montréal, Québec, Canada
www.vehiculepress.com

Distribution in Canada by LitDistCo
www.litdistco.ca

Distributed in the U.S. by Independent Publishers Group
www.ipgbook.com

Printed in Canada on FSC certified paper

For Archie

Contents

"History is mystery."

–Marisa Silver, interviewed by Eleanor Wachtel,
Writers & Company

Preface

"WERE THERE ANY black sheep in the Notman family?"
It was an idle interview question. I had just begun research for a CBC
Ideas radio documentary on William Notman. Notman was among
Canada's finest nineteenth-century photographers, the first to achieve
international renown, and the most commercially successful of all
North American photographers of his time. He had, in addition, an
interesting personal history. But as I sat facing Nora Hague, the senior expert on all things Notman at Montreal's McCord Museum, I
wasn't deliberately fishing. I was simply doing what a writer does au-
tomatically, sniffing around for possible material.

"Well," she said, "there was his brother, John. Also a photographer, who was run over by a train. He had what today is called a
drinking problem…." She paused. Picking her words carefully, she
added, "And of course there was Robert, another hard-living boy.
The brother who was tried for murder…. A huge case that was reported in all its ins-and-outs in the *Gazette*…." Her voice trailed off.
I had the distinct impression that this chapter of the Notman saga
was strictly classified.

While conducting my official study of Notman's career, I started
to poke around the story of the murderous brother. And stumbled on
a tale far more intriguing than a gothic whodunit. A drama through
which Victorian Montreal, so lavishly depicted by the camera of
William Notman, may be viewed beneath the surface of carefully
arranged settings, heroic poses, and gorgeous costumes. A story with
themes that travel well across generations and cultures: the flouting
of society's rules and its consequences.

There was no murder, but there was illicit sex, abortion, suicide,
a trial. It was a big story and so difficult to research that I gave up
working on it several times. Too much of the source material derived
from smudged editions of newspapers on microfilm. Too much of
it was couched in nineteenth-century legal palaver. But even as I
contorted my back over the microfilm reader and strained my eyes
trying to decipher poorly reproduced pages of ancient newsprint,
the story would not let go of me. There was the famous brother and

his estimable wife, and the other brother in whose wake tragedy inevitably followed.

In *The Story of Chicago May*, Irish writer Nuala O'Faolain muses about the great anonymity that surrounds the vast majority of the millions of people who have in their time walked the Earth. She laments that as a consequence of that obscurity, an "enormous amount of what the world once contained is lost." By reconstructing the story of the notorious Irish-American criminal Chicago May, O'Faolain felt that she had recovered "an atom of history."

This is also how I feel about the story you are about to read, though it differs markedly from that of Chicago May. May courted celebrity and thrived on her sensational reputation as a bad girl. Margaret Galbraith and Robert Notman – the couple at the heart of this book – courted secrecy. Though they were unmasked in the most public of ways, their private story remains veiled.

Most of this book is written as straight history and is primarily a work of non-fiction. But as in my previous historical works, I have felt free to imagine and speculate where motivations and events are unknown or unclear, emboldening myself with the thought that even if I knew much more of the historical record, ultimately I would not unlock all mysteries. Many of these imagined passages are marked in italics in the text, but to use italics a great deal can be distracting for readers. I trust therefore that it will be clear that when I write of the thoughts and feelings of my characters, these interpretations are my intuitions, not hard facts.

What I have aimed for is a snapshot of a particular society at a particular moment. Wherever possible, I have allowed the characters to speak in their own words as reported by the press of the day. Some of the trial evidence is reconstructed dialogue; however, everything within quotation marks is derived verbatim from those reports.

When it comes to the subject of abortion, I was surprised to learn that it was a much larger phenomenon in the nineteenth century than I had supposed. I have tried to present it in the context of its own day, and not within the framework of heated contemporary pro-choice and right-to-life rhetoric.

Prologue

Summer 1867, 3 Eliot Terrace, St. Catherine Street.

He brushes against her in the corridor. She backs away, instinctively shrinking from contact. She is a servant in this household, knows her place.

Another time, he stubs his toe, pitching forward as he tails her in the hallway. Again she recoils, so eager to flatten – even erase – herself that through the thin stuff of her blouse she can feel the nub of the rose-embossed wallpaper against her shoulder blades.

Her modesty inflames him. Were she a tart, she'd hold little appeal. Or if her comportment were more in tune with her appearance, he might be content to pinch her bottom and toss her a debonair smile. But it's the contrast between her bold good looks and mousey manners that excites him. She is a handsome woman, broad-shouldered, straight-backed, wide-hipped, a strong country girl, the kind that's needed to help his mother with his father's ablutions and bath chair.

He craves to dissolve her reserve, unlock the secret cry that a woman shrieks when it goes well with her. When she abandons herself.

What the French of this city call la jouissance.

CHAPTER ONE

A Sudden Death

Montreal, February 26, 1868

IN SUMMER IT WAS A CITY of melons, strawberries, and sweet corn grown in backyards and bucolic outskirts, while downtown streets hummed with sidewalk vendors touting ice cream and cool drinks to a perspiring public garbed in the tight stays and high collars dictated by propriety.

But winter was its true calling, its season par excellence. It was a city of snow, ice, and tinkling sleigh bells, built on the banks of a river with prodigious currents. Every year the St. Lawrence froze solidly enough to form a bridge of ice linking the island of Montreal to the mainland. A pathway marked by fir branches guided travellers along the treacherous route of irregular slopes and snow dunes along the ice.

It was a city of domes and spires – "a mountain of churches," wrote Harriet Beecher Stowe. An actual, if small, mountain rose at its heart and bore Maisonneuve's historic cross. You could shoot foxes on that mountain, or toboggan downs its flanks, or scale it on snowshoes by torchlight.

As a place to live, it was hardly idyllic: a city of ice shoves, ice jams, and spring floods, of cholera and smallpox. Its wooden sidewalks were hazardous and dirty, it was prone to fire, and its plumbing was a disaster. For several days in a row at the end of February that particular year, ice up river blocked the aqueduct near the Lachine Rapids, depleting the reservoir on the mountainside and leaving the city without running water. Indignant editorials pointed out that the "water works" of a city of 100,000 consisted of navvies carting barrels drawn from the river and delivering them to households where they had to be purchased by the tin pail. And if the stench in water closets and the risk of fire weren't bad enough, railed the *Gazette*, some of the water carriers were filling their puncheons from holes in the ice "close to the wharves and below the College Street sewer outlet – one of the filthiest drains in the city."

It was a city of social, linguistic, religious, and architectural disparities. It had streets of squalid frame huts that reminded one Montrealer of "an Irishman's hovel on his native bog." But the shacks stood in the shadow of "great streets of great houses, all of fine-cut stone." This indigenous grey limestone resembled the building blocks of parts of France and Scotland, a likeness that must have been comforting to those of its many citizens of French and Scots heritage.

It was a city of fur barons and clergymen, of nuns and belles, of British garrison officers, merchants, factory owners and labourers. The word multicultural would not be coined for another century and yet the reality of ethnic diversity already stamped this city. On its streets strolled offspring of the early French settlers and more recently arrived inhabitants from England, Ireland, and Scotland. St. Lawrence Street marked its linguistic divide: to the east lived "thousands of French who [could] not speak one word of English," to the west "thousands of English who [could] not speak one word of French." English and French had to share the city with, among others, the "unmistakable descendants of the ancient Iroquois Indians," and even more exotic minorities. A few days before our story begins, the Jews of the English and German Synagogue on St. Constant Street (the precursor of the Congregation Shaar Hashomayim) inaugurated a new Torah scroll in an elaborate ceremony reported in fulsome detail by an awestruck reporter for the *Gazette*.

It was a city like and unlike other cities in and out of its time, peopled by individuals cast in their own specificity, possessing their own unique dreams and terrors.

Two such were James Benning and Dr. Alfred Patton.

Feeling unwell on the evening of February 26 – a Wednesday – the former called upon the latter. Eight o'clock wasn't too late to ring the doctor's doorbell – the address on Craig Street was both office and residence – but in any case, as Mr. Benning would later testify at the inquest, he'd been in the habit of going to see Dr. Patton, "as I was intimate with him."

He did not mean "intimate" in an erotic sense, but rather of close connection or friendship. As a token of that intimacy, the two men enjoyed a little rye whiskey together, Dr. Patton adding a splash of water to his own drink, and infusing that of Mr. Benning with three drops of morphine. This, he assured him, would make him "all right." Mr. Benning would have found nothing untoward in the prescription, opiates being among the most common of medications of the day.

Later, perhaps to clear their heads, they set out for a constitutional, but ventured only as far and back as the short distance to the St. Lawrence Hall Hotel, a couple of snow-humped streets west and south of Dr. Patton's place. By now it was eleven o'clock, and Mr. Benning proposed returning to his own home. Dr. Patton pressed him to stay on. He still had a couple of late-night calls to make, one of them at the St. Lawrence Hall, but if Mr. Benning stayed on, the doctor could look after him at night if need be, as he had done on previous occasions.

Mr. Benning didn't need urging. The two men returned to the doctor's house and Benning penned a few quick lines to his business partner, Joseph Barsalou ("to tell where I was"). He gave the note to Dr. Patton to deliver.

Upstairs, Jane Dacey, the housekeeper's daughter, heard the whoosh of the runners as the doctor's sleigh pulled away, but Mr. Benning – overcome by the rye and morphine cocktail – fell instantly asleep on the sofa in the parlour.

Beyond the fact that James Benning was a partner in the firm of Benning & Barsalou, Auctioneers and Commission Agents on Peter Street, that he resided at the Ottawa Hotel on Great St. James Street, and that he was a patient and friend of Dr. Patton, little is known of him. Since he notified his partner and not a wife that he'd be staying out all night, it's unlikely that there was a Mrs. Benning in the picture.

Of pictures of Mr. Benning himself there are two, both taken at Montreal's renowned Notman Studio, coincidentally in 1868. They depict an open countenanced, portly man with a full beard and bushy moustache, light coloured eyes, and curly hair slicked back from a high forehead. He had an affable gaze and surprisingly relaxed stance for someone suffering from an anxiety disorder – the condition for which, his testimony at the inquest suggests, Dr. Patton was treating him. When the doctor took his leave for his late-night calls, Mr. Benning later informed the Coroner, "he told me if I felt nervous to come into his room when I awoke."

At around midnight, the doorbell rang twice at 494 Lagauchetiere Street. Emerging groggily from sleep, Joseph Barsalou tried to gather his wits. On the doorstep, Dr. Patton pushed Mr. Benning's note through the mail slot, and – impatient to be off – turned on his heel. Upstairs, snug beneath his coverlet, Mr. Barsalou interpreted the fading chime of sleigh bells and muted pounding of hooves on snow as the departure of his mystery caller. He did not bother to get out of bed, but rolled over and went back to sleep.

Dr. Patton had told Mr. Benning that he needed to see two patients. One of them remains anonymous. The other resided at the St. Lawrence Hall. Likely Dr. Patton visited the anonymous patient before he arrived at Mr. Barsalou's on Lagauchetiere Street, and possibly this patient lived nearby. This could account for the interval between eleven o'clock, when Dr. Patton left his home, and midnight when he arrived at Mr. Barsalou's, a mere two streets north of Craig Street.

Jane Dacey, the housekeeper's daughter, later testified that the doctor arrived back home at three in the morning of Thursday, February 27. Even allowing a generous half hour for the short distances covered by him in his sleigh, he must have spent two and a half hours by the bedside of his patient at the St. Lawrence Hall.

The St. Lawrence Hall stood at the north west corner of Great St. James and St. François Xavier streets, near Place d'Armes "in the most salubrious and fashionable part of the City," according to its advertisement in *The Canada Directory*. Centrally located opposite the Bank of British North America, with nearby access to the post office, telegraph office, and the principal businesses of the city, it was Montreal's finest hotel. It prided itself on its cuisine, concert room, and hot and cold water baths. Boasting of furnishings "in the best style of the New York and Boston hotels," it claimed to be "Unequalled by any Hotel in Canada." A few years back it had been known as a haven for Confederate spies, and was in 1868 heavily patronized by wealthy American and British tourists.

The lady occupying the suite composed of rooms 103 and 104 on the ground floor came neither from New York nor London, but from a rooming house on Lagauchetiere Street. Dr. Patton had been treating her with a variety of remedies for the past ten weeks. What transpired between her, Dr. Patton, and Mr. Robert Notman – the younger brother of William Notman, self-styled and extremely successful "Photographer to the Queen" – became "the affair in everybody's mouth," English-speaking Montreal's *cause célèbre* of the winter and spring of 1868.

At 564 Craig Street, Jane Dacey heard Dr. Patton return home. She recognized his step, heard him remove his boots, and throw them down. She fell back to sleep.

James Benning came out of his slumber at about quarter past four. A folding door separating the parlour from Dr. Patton's bedroom at the back of the house had been left ajar. A coal oil lamp which Benning had deliberately left on was still flickering and flaring in the parlour, and, as he rose from the sofa, its pale light illuminated the face of Dr. Patton in the adjoining room.

Benning had been instructed to address himself to Dr. Patton if he woke in the night and he now did as directed. "I went into his room and sat down on the side of his bed," Mr. Benning testified. "His one hand was sticking up and I felt his hand was deathly cold. To make sure, I took hold of his whisker to turn his face over, and found him dead."

Montreal Gazette, Friday, February 28, 1868
SUDDEN DEATH

We regret to have to record the sudden death of Alfred Patton, Esq., M.D., formerly of Beech Lodge, Castlerea [*sic*], Belfast, County Down, Ireland, under painful circumstances. The deceased formerly occupied the position of surgeon on board several of the vessels of the Montreal Ocean Steamship Company in which capacity he was much esteemed by all; but in October 1867 he opened an office at No. 564, Craig Street, near Place D'Armes Hill, and soon began to do a fair practice. On Wednesday evening he was observed to be perfectly well up to about 11 o'clock, and had spent the latter portion of a the evening in his room with Mr. James Benning, of the firm of

Benning and Barsalou. The deceased occupied the front and back room on the ground floor, on the left side of the hall, the two rooms being separated by folding doors, and the back room being used as bedroom. He also kept his medicines there, on a sideboard and in a closet. The deceased appears to have ultimately retired to his bedroom, and his companion, Mr. James Benning, it is stated, went to sleep on the sofa in the front room. About 4 o'clock yesterday morning [Thursday], Mr. Benning rose and going into the back room found Dr. Patton was lying dead on his bed. The deceased had dressed himself in his night clothes very neatly, which in the morning appeared not to have been disturbed. He was found lying on his right side in a natural position, his face rather inclined inward, and the bed clothes comfortably tucked under him. Mr. Benning, we understand, immediately went to inform his partner, Mr. Barsalou, and thereupon information was given to Chief Penton, of the City Police, who immediately had the Coroner notified. Yesterday morning at 11 o'clock, Mr. Coroner Jones empanelled a most respectable jury at the late residence of the deceased,… and summoned Doctors Craik and Howard… and the medical men stated that it would be necessary to hold a Post Mortem examination…. In conclusion we may state the deceased had made many friends in Montreal and was esteemed by all who knew him. The funeral will take place at one o'clock on Saturday.

A popular young man – the *Herald* gave his age as "about thirty" – esteemed by all who knew him, dead under distressing circumstances. Distressing not only for him but also for all those who knew him, and none more so than poor, traumatized Mr. Benning. Within days an inquest would only further mystify a perplexed public.

CHAPTER TWO

Medical Gentlemen

THOUGH IT WAS CANADA's largest city at the time of Confederation, Montreal still retained characteristics of a village. When Messrs. Benning and Barsalou decided to search for the police chief, they knew to find him either at home at 76 St. Denis Street, or at the police station in Bonsecours Market. Chief Frederick Penton then notified the Coroner, and by eleven o'clock on Thursday morning, Coroner Joseph Jones had assembled a jury of fourteen men in the home of the deceased. Their first order of business was to recruit two eminent physicians to determine the cause of death.

Doctors Robert Craik and Robert Palmer Howard were both native Montrealers born in the 1820s whose careers ran in remarkable tandem. Both attended McGill University; Dr. Howard graduated in 1848 and Dr. Craik in 1854 (with the highest honours in his year). Dr. Howard took postgraduate studies in Dublin, London, Edinburgh, and Paris, while Dr. Craik was appointed House Surgeon at the Montreal General straight out of school. Both became professors at McGill and practised at the Montreal General, its teaching hospital. Each had a sterling reputation as a teacher; each would eventually become Dean of the Faculty of Medicine. Dr. Howard, in particular, was known as a superb lecturer, his scholarship grounded in both extensive clinical experience and rigorous post-mortem examinations.

The great William Osler, often called the Father of Modern Medicine, studied and later worked with both men at McGill, and frequently acknowledged Howard as an influential teacher. ("I have never known one in whom was more happily combined a stern sense of duty with the mental freshness of youth," he said of Howard.) Osler thought considerably less highly of Dr. Craik. "He has no notion of the needs of anything but a stud horse & a brood mare," he wrote to a friend in 1884. The disparaging allusion was to Craik's great hobby. Widowed at the age of forty-five and childless, he developed a passion for animal husbandry. (A three-year-old bay stallion called Harbinger, "bred by Dr. Craik,

Montreal," took the ten-dollar second prize at an Ontario agricultural fair in 1866; "Dr. Craik's Cattle" is the title of a series of Notman photographs of bovines at pasture.)

The two distinguished physicians examined Dr. Patton's body for external marks of violence. This likely took place in the back bedroom, while the jury and presiding Coroner must have crowded together in the parlour. In relatively short order, the doctors reported back that the corpse bore no signs of violence; they would have to perform an autopsy. The Coroner therefore adjourned the inquest, calling the jury back for three that afternoon. At the appointed hour, the physicians once more asked for an extension. To come up with a definitive answer they would have to analyze the contents of the dead man's stomach. Coroner Jones gave them a couple of extra days, adjourning the proceedings until Saturday afternoon at four.

At the appointed hour, Dr. Craik, the younger man, acted as spokesman for "the medical gentlemen." Craggily handsome with a high brow, deepset eyes, and firm set to his chin, he was at this time professor of clinical surgery and of chemistry at McGill. He launched into a meticulous itemization of the findings.

He didn't mind admitting that when he and Dr. Howard had begun their examination the previous day, they "did so without the least idea of the cause of death." Their first finding was a "slight odour of alcohol exhaled from the mouth of the deceased, and a scarcely perceptible trace in the brain." After the head, they scrutinized the heart, lungs and liver, "and all the internal organs" in turn, finding them all consistent with those of a man of health and "in a natural state except [for] venous congestion."

It was when they analyzed the stomach that they located their prime clue. "The stomach, after having been carefully removed, was found to contain about four ounces of a semi-fluid substance, which was placed in a clean basin." (It's well to remember the shortage of water in the city at this time. Cleanliness must not have been easy to come by.) At first they suspected the unknown substance to be alcohol, but on smelling it "were immediately struck with the presence of the odour of prussic acid, the first thing that could give any indication of the cause of death."

What the medical gentlemen had sniffed was the faint, burnt-almond bitterness of hydrogen cyanide, a colourless, highly volatile, and extremely poisonous liquid. Commonly called prussic acid because the Swedish scientist who discovered it in the late eighteenth century extracted it from a blue dye called Prussian blue, it has beneficial industrial applications to this day. Despite the fact that an overdose could halt cellular respiration, bringing on near-instant death, in the nineteenth century it was used as a therapeutic sedative. Of course its sinister future could not then be fathomed. In gas form, released from Zyklon B pellets, hydrogen cyanide was the agent employed in Nazi concentration camps for the purpose of mass murder. It has also been used in certain parts of the United States for judicial execution.

As far as the doctors were concerned, the discovery of prussic acid in the dead man's stomach broke the case. A little later they detected traces of the poison "in the blood from the heart.... The post-mortem appearances were quite reconcilable with the presence of prussic acid, the most noticeable features being the general congestion of the organs, and the liquid condition and dark colour of the blood usual in poisoning by prussic acid."

In being so forthright about the graphic details of the autopsy, the *Gazette* and the *Herald* – the two papers that covered the inquest closely – seemed confident of their readers' avid interest and strong stomachs. Though they were writing for the general public and not an esoteric medical audience, they seemed blithely insensitive to standards imposed by what we today would call "family values." This was an audience that didn't have recourse to *Grey's Anatomy, ER,* or *In Treatment.* For information and entertainment, they turned to newspapers, books, plays, and concerts. But for immediacy and juicy content, nothing rivalled the daily papers.

The rest of Dr. Craik's testimony was tamer. Having arrived at a cause of death, he and Dr. Howard next turned their attention to searching for the source of the poison. On the sideboard in the bedroom where Dr. Patton kept his apothecary supplies, they found "amongst the other vials, a common-ounce vial containing about 40 minims of ordinary prussic acid.... Only an approximation of the quantity could be given, from one to two drams having been probably taken."

In the measurement of a dosage of medicine, a minim represents 1/480 of an imperial fluid ounce or one sixtieth of a fluid dram, a dram being an eighth of a fluid ounce. The *Gazette* helpfully calculated for its readers. "The deceased must have taken one or two teaspoonfuls, equal to one or two drams."

In answer to a question from the coroner and jury, Dr. Craik found nothing remarkable in Dr. Patton having the drug in his possession, since prussic acid "as a medicine … is taken to allay vomiting and to relieve pains and cramps in the stomach and is sometimes given as a general sedative for the nerves."

The questions turned to the length of time death might follow a fatal dose. The doctor estimated the range to be from two to ten minutes. "In the case of a strong, healthy man, like [the] deceased, insensibility would probably supervene in about two minutes, and death shortly after. Insensibility has been known to follow in ten seconds."

A discussion followed about the manner in which the drug was taken and whether the death was suicide or an accidental overdose. "If any one had premeditated suicide," Dr. Craik mused, "he could pour the poison in another vessel, take it to the bedside, pour it into his mouth, but not swallow it till he had arranged everything about him. The poison would act, but not so rapidly as if swallowed [immediately]."

Asked if Dr. Patton might have taken the drug standing by the medicine table, Dr. Craik replied, "It is possible he might have swallowed it at the table. [But] I believe the poison was taken in bed."

– If Dr. Patton had taken prussic acid for pain, in what manner would he have ingested it?

"If taken to alleviate pains he would have taken it in bed in the same way."

– And what would then have been the dose?

"From one to five drops is the usual dose in such cases."

– But how could an experienced practitioner make such a mistake? Confound five drops with three drams?

Dr. Craik's response to this question was extraordinary.

"It is possible that, from the habit of dispensing medicine, deceased might have undervalued the strength of the poison, and rashly taken more than he ought to have done, and he would be more probably rash in his own case than in that of his patients." In other words, as the proverbial shoemaker's children go barefoot, so a physician will be reckless with his own health.

– Was there anything still remaining on the sideboard when you examined it?

"A bottle of Stoughton Bitters was … close to the bottle of Prussic Acid, on the sideboard…. There was another tumbler on the medicine table one-third full of whiskey and water."

– Did the tumbler by the bedside contain prussic acid?

"I examined … [it, but] it seemed to have contained nothing but water; it might have contained prussic acid, but being a volatile substance, all traces of it would have had time to disappear…."

– Can you account for the excessive amount of prussic acid taken by Dr. Patton?

"The quantity taken might have been poured out carelessly, and as the mouth of the vials sometimes prevents the liquid from flowing freely, more might suddenly run out than was intended."

– Could the alcohol you found in the body have caused intoxication?

"The alcohol was not sufficient to cause intoxication."

– Might the dose of prussic acid have been administered by force to Dr. Patton?

"That is out of the question. The dose could not have been given against his will. A small quantity, in spirits and water, might have been swallowed without being noticed."

– In conclusion, can you say how much prussic acid was ingested?

"What remains in the bottle, deducted from the total quantity purchased would show that about three drams had been used."

When the jury foreman inquired if Dr. Howard had anything to add, he confirmed the evidence of his colleague. However, Dr. Howard said that he believed it was quite possible for Dr. Patton to have taken the dose by the sideboard and have time to walk back to bed and arrange himself for sleep in the position in which he was found. "Even if he took it as medicine for pains in the stomach, and particularly if he had taken it in spirits, this could be done. There were a number of vials besides this one, and it was quite likely that he had mistaken this for another."

Both doctors thus implied that death had been accidental. Dr. Craik believed that either Dr. Patton had been carelessly self-medicating, or that an excess of the drug had poured out of the bottle, escaping the victim's notice if he took it as an analgesic with alcohol. Dr. Howard suggested he might accidentally have taken the wrong bottle.

A parade of non-expert witnesses was called next, James Benning being first. In addition to recounting the events of his evening with Dr. Patton and his subsequent discovery of the body, he said that he had seen nothing to indicate that the doctor was troubled in any way. "He appeared satisfied with his business prospects. That night he left me he was perfectly sober, and his manner was quite natural."

Jane Dacey recounted the story of the doctor's comings and goings as she discerned them upstairs, where she lived with her mother. She too commented that "he spoke quite politely and naturally" to her when he requested that she make up a room in the house for a friend. She noted that "the room I had prepared had not been slept in, but the blanket and comforter had been taken downstairs," this fact tying in with Mr. Benning's account of sleeping on the sofa in the parlour, to be close to Dr. Patton.

John Taylor, whose wife was a patient of Dr. Patton, testified that he saw the doctor at twenty past eight on Wednesday evening at the St. Lawrence Hall, when he was "perfectly sober." Mr. Taylor lauded Dr. Patton's bedside manner as "very kind and cheerful." On Wednesday evening "we had conversations about his prospects, and he seemed very hopeful."

Alfred Boulter had spent time with Dr. Patton on Tuesday evening when the two had had a glass of rye together. This must have occurred at the doctor's, since Mr. Boulter said that "in the glass taken by each, deceased put a little bitters, taken from the place where all the other phials were taken."

At this point Dr. Craik interjected that "it would be well for him to mention that, standing close to where the prussic acid phial was found, there was a bottle of tincture of gentian, similar to Stoughton Bitters." Boulter must have jogged the doctor's memory. Tincture of gentian was a "tonic and stomachic" used for both dyspepsia and hysteria. Dr. Craik clearly wanted to underline his thesis that Dr.

Patton had digestive ailments.

A rambling and disjointed testimony from Edward C. Ward, who took his meals with Dr. Patton at a neighbouring rooming house, alluded to a dinnertime conversation with him a month earlier during which they had discussed "various modes of death and symptoms of poisoning by prussic acid."

The last witness to be called was Police Chief Frederick W.L. Penton. His testimony was terse but vivid. He described the position in which he found the body after he had been fetched by Messrs. Benning and Barsalou. He had tried to turn the corpse over, but it was already stiff. However, "the head was warm, as if death had been recent. On a chair by the side of the bed was an empty tumbler and water jug. There was not the slightest smell from the tumbler. There was a tumbler with some whiskey and water in it on the drawers, but it did not appear to have been drunk out of."

The jury conferred only a short time before pronouncing the verdict. They concluded that "the said Alfred Patton came to his death by taking a quantity of prussic acid." They had not been swayed by the medical gentlemen's subtle pressure to return a verdict of accidental death. They declared themselves unable to say whether the poison had been taken intentionally or accidentally.

In the meantime, Chief Penton, a man of few words, kept silent about the fresh line of investigation he had begun. That was Saturday. By the following Wednesday morning his findings were splashed across the city's major English papers.

CHAPTER THREE

The Whole Affair

BENEATH THE HEADLINE "Crime and Suicide," a front-page editorial in the Montreal *Herald* on Wednesday, March 4, 1868 debunked the theory of accidental death in its first sentence.

> The difficulty of comprehending the suicide of the late Dr. Patton and forming an argument as to how far his taking of the Prussic acid, which caused his death, was due to accident or design, seems likely to be cleared up in a very painful manner.

Fresh evidence uncovered by the police, the paper stated, suggested that Dr. Patton had participated in a crime. "The intelligent reader of the report of the inquest" must have wondered about Dr. Patton's mysterious activities between eleven at night and three in the morning. "It seems now too certain that he was engaged in a very serious offence, which apparently had consequences much more fatal than he had expected, and that in his remorse he executed with his own hand the penalty which outraged society might have exacted at a later day."

According to the *Herald*, the police had discovered that the doctor had performed an abortion, and "by that wicked and dangerous practice, he had brought the unfortunate woman with whose life he was tampering, to the point of death." The paper floated the hypothesis that "he probably believed ... he had left her dead from the effects of the chloroform which he had administered; and he went straight home, and thence, probably within a very few minutes, launched himself into that unknown eternity, whither he supposed that he had just sent his victim."

The writer pondered about the implications of what the doctor may have done. "By what temptation a man, who could feel such deep and sudden remorse, could be led to break through all the safeguards drawn round him by professional etiquette, as well as by moral considerations, we perhaps shall never know." But Dr. Patton's experience was an "additional warning ... of the wretchedness and misery" resulting from such actions. And then the editorialist dropped a second bombshell. "After all, his self-condemnation has, perhaps, been the only one which could have fallen upon him, as the unfortunate girl, in whose case he foully misapplied the knowledge he had obtained for noble ends, was not dead as he supposed. The effects of the anaesthesia have passed, and she is believed to be recovering from the consequences of the treatment to which she was subjected."

The *Gazette*'s treatment of the story was considerably less high flown. In lieu of moralizing, it had sensational details to impart, and it ran them beneath a headline and two breathless subheads.

THE RECENT DEATH OF DR. PATTON
STRANGE CIRCUMSTANCES CONNECTED
THEREWITH
AN ABORTION CASE AT THE ST. LAWRENCE HALL AND
WHAT CAME OF IT

Some facts transpired yesterday which give strong ground for the suspicion so freely entertained that Dr. Patton deliberately poisoned himself, and was not, as some supposed, the victim of an accident which appeared to be unaccountable in a medical man, accustomed to handle phials and aware of the nature and properties of medicines. The authorities are very reticent yet, although the whole affair is in everybody's mouth, but the following facts transpired in the course of yesterday.

Hot on the police's trail – or with solid contacts in the force – the *Gazette* reporter was all over the story, handily scooping his colleague at the *Herald*. He named names, one of which would likely resonate with his readers. "It appears that Mr. Robert Notman, of this city, seduced a girl named Galbraith some time ago."

The reporter, or his editor, had so little consideration or sympathy for the girl in question as to omit according her the honourific of "Miss." "The first intimation of the affair was that Galbraith was missing from her boarding house…." Since inquiries made at the homes of her friends yielded no information, "the assistance of a detective was obtained." The *Gazette* didn't disclose who was responsible for bringing a detective on board, but in the course of his sleuthing someone decided to search a trunk belonging to the girl. Letters in it were "said to implicate Mr. R. Notman."

In addition to casting suspicion on Robert Notman, these letters would be material evidence at a forthcoming trial, and – down the road – the manner in which they were made public would have serious repercussions for the case.

> It was at last discovered that she had been taken to the St. Lawrence Hall, where for some days certain drugs had been unsuccessfully administered to her, and eventually an operation is said to have been performed on her the effect of which reduced her to such a state of distress and exhaustion that her life was despaired of, and this preying on Dr. Patton's mind, induced him, there is now reason to believe, to commit suicide….
>
> We have heard the Chief of Police afterwards received private information of the facts and of the girl being at the St. Lawrence Hall. The whole of the attendant circumstances were speedily discovered, and Mr. Notman was arrested and lodged in jail, charged with procuring an abortion.

Chief Penton had been busy. Head of a chronically understaffed and underpaid police force, he was forever beseeching the city administration for additional funds and resources. Nonetheless he had found a culprit, was building a case against him, and had clapped him in jail. Given the shortcomings of his staff, the "private information" to which the *Gazette* alluded must have been crucial.

Until Lord Durham established one in wake of the 1837 rebellions, Montreal didn't have a police force at all, but made do with a nightwatch patrol scouting for outbreaks of fire. But once created, the new force was nearly useless. In 1849 when an angry mob protested against the implementation of the Rebellion Losses Bill and burned down the Parliament buildings (which at the time were housed in

Montreal), a contingent of some seventy men (for a city of 50,000) stood helpless before the insurgents.

By the 1860s the force had grown to 150, but the population had also more than doubled. Chief Penton, who took charge in 1865, had his work cut out. But he was a talented and dedicated administrator, who rose to the challenge. Born in Calais, France, in 1826 and educated on the Island of Jersey, he was completely bilingual, the son of a French mother and English father. Before taking on the police department, he served three years as the Superintendent of the City Passenger Railway, Montreal's horse-drawn tram company. A small glimmer of light on his private life shows him a steward of the Montreal Snow Shoe Club.

In the Notman photo of him taken in 1863, Chief Penton wears a workman's jacket and trousers, and carries a bowler. He has an intelligent gaze and a look of dogged patience. He needed both brains and fortitude for his new assignment. In 1873 he would plead eloquently with the municipal authorities for better wages for his men. "It is hardly possible to expect that really able and strong men can be kept in the Force for the paltry sum of eight dollars a week," he wrote. Manual labourers whom "no one expects … to be men of sound judgment or of bodily courage" were paid two or two-fifty a day, "while subconstables who are required to be sober, intelligent and stoutly built, to be ready at all times for duty, in fair or foul weather, day and night, during the extreme summer heat and severe cold of the winter months … only receive from the public a poor salary of $8 a week."

No wonder then, argued the chief, that it was impossible to achieve continuity of service. Men were using the force "as a kind of stepping stone, or rather waiting platform until something better shall turn up." The force continued to be short staffed "for the simple reason that the wages are not considered sufficient to support a family even in the most humble and economical manner."

To the favourite cry of the public of "where's the police?", Chief Penton retorted that "the Police are doing duty on their several and respective beats, but as disturbers of the peace, thieves and rowd[ies] are not in the habit of plying their nefarious avocations when a policeman is in sight, it is impossible for the constables to be at every spot along their beats…."

In other words, a Montreal constable's lot – like that of the police sergeant in Gilbert and Sullivan's *Pirates of Penzance* – was not a happy one. But it was, in a manner of speaking, a rather happy circumstance to be able to explain the mysterious circumstances of Dr. Patton's demise, find a suspect in a related crime, and appear exceedingly competent with one fell swoop. And already, less than a week after the doctor's death, the *Gazette* had the main outlines of the story in place.

Mr. Brehaut, Police Magistrate, began to take the necessary depositions yesterday, and first proceeded to examine the girl Galbraith at the St. Lawrence Hall. She occupies room No. 103, on one of the most public passages of the hotel, and is said to have been educated at the Normal School of this city. She testified that Dr. Patton had committed an abortion upon her, that she was delivered at 7 o'clock on the morning previous to his death; that the child she gave birth to, as well as the after birth, were removed in a bucket by the doctor; and that she had been seduced and brought to the hotel by Mr. Notman. She was very weak, but able to sit up and sign her deposition, and it is believed will soon recover.

Once again, the explicit nature of the reporting confounds the popular stereotype of the prudish Victorian. The image of the doctor disposing of the tiny foetus with its closed eyes and neatly folded limbs along with the bloody placenta lingers in the mind. What is also riveting is that the reference to the bucket never surfaced in the extensive reporting that was yet to come. Nor was there ever again mention of Miss Galbraith attending the McGill Normal School – a fact without which it would be almost impossible to begin to reconstruct her life.

Further depositions will be taken today [March 4], among others that of Dr. Campbell, the medical man who was requested to make an examination in order to establish whether an abortion had been committed, as also the woman who attended Miss Galbraith during her confinement. Mr. Devlin has been retained on behalf of the defence.

By March 5, the papers were referring to the story as "The Abortion Case," and covering it on a nearly daily basis. On March 7, the *Gazette* reported that Miss Galbraith was being kept under surveillance, lest she flee. That same day, *La Minerve,* an influential Montreal French paper, ran a translation of the *Gazette*'s March 4 article verbatim. It concluded with the sentence "M. Devlin doit prendre la défense," to which it tacked on an observation of its own: "Un tel fait n'a pas besoin de commentaire." Bernard Devlin was a seasoned criminal lawyer with twenty years experience. *La Minerve* was implying that Notman was in the deepest of trouble.

The scandalmongers' tongues were wagging at high speed, since the *Gazette* felt compelled to clear up a certain misconception. "Yesterday Robert Notman was finally committed for trial at the approaching term of the Court of Queen's Bench on three distinct terms of abortion. The person committed is not the well-known photographer, whose name is William Notman."

CHAPTER FOUR

The Well-known Photographer
1856

WHEN THE WELL-KNOWN photographer arrived in Montreal in 1856, he was neither well-known, nor a real photographer. In his native Scotland he had been engaged in a completely different line of work. Failure and discredit brought him to the shores of the St. Lawrence at the age of thirty.

The descendant of a long line of coal-mining and farming William Notmans, who had originated in the Midlothian district of south-eastern Scotland, our William was born in 1826 into a prosperous, upwardly-mobile family in the town of Paisley, a stone's throw west of Glasgow.

He appears to have enjoyed a contented, almost idyllic child-hood. One of his earliest memories was of being taken to a farm to visit his grandfather, "a fine old man with lots of hair and beard ….and sitting on his knee and playing with his watch." This hir-sute old William Notman, called a "Cowfeeder" – or dairyman – had moved the family westwards to Paisley in the early nineteenth cen-tury, when a major agricultural dislocation was forcing farmers off the land. The Cowfeeder put a priority on education, so that the future photographer's father, the one we'll call William Senior, was well educated. According to family lore, William Senior loved school so much that his bride "paid his last quarter fee at school so she could get him free to be married."

William Senior became a merchant and entrepreneur, but he also had an artistic bent. A textile centre of note, Paisley had a pop-ulation of 50,000, and was the third largest city in Scotland. It was famous for the popular fashion accessory called "the Paisley shawl" whose elaborate motifs were developed there. William Senior de-signed many of the gorgeous patterns himself and marketed the finished product that cottagers wove in their homes for him.

When the future photographer was about fourteen, William Senior suffered a business reverse: the Paisley shawl fell out of favour. The Notmans moved to Glasgow, where William Senior eventually became a dry goods wholesaler, a related occupation in textiles, notions, and ready-made clothing at which he prospered. Our William obtained a classical education that he didn't seem to much appreciate; many years later in Montreal he disparaged "the routine of school and the tedium of Greek and Latin exercises."

In interviews after he became famous, Notman said that he had studied art for several years in his youth. Without a doubt, he possessed a painterly eye and sensibility. Among his papers lie notes for a speech in which he summoned up memories of seaside holidays in Kilmun, a little village in Argyllshire that overlooks Holy Loch, a sea loch open to the Firth of Clyde. Notman recalled rising with the sun to accompany a Gaelic-speaking shepherd called Archie to inspect "the fleecy flocks scattered here and there over the mountainside...." He wrote of "meeting the perfumed breeze as it danced over the waving heather," of descending the mountain through a veil of clouds, and then of seeing, hundreds of feet below, "the loch placid and bright as a mirror with many fishing boats lining the shore, some at anchor, some drawn up on the beach, nets hung out to dry...."

After breakfast – "and the usual bible reading" – came further adventures in the company of brothers and sisters. Duncan McNeil, the ferryman ,"a man of many years, fond of bairns, weather-beaten, weatherwise, full of yarns from the sea, bald headed, with a blue bonnet, a shaggy beard, fond of his pipe – and not averse at times to a drop of mountain dew," took them sailing. The quaint home of the so-called Hermit of Kilmun, a mile uphill from the village, was another favourite destination. Unusual for the countryside, the Hermit's door was always barred, so that visitors had to knock. "Inside everything was neat and tidy, his old gun which when in good humour he was fond of shewing, rested above the fireplace, his cupboards ... models of neatness considering that he allowed no feminine hand to interfere with his household arrangements."

From these tantalizingly scarce jottings, Notman comes across as having keen powers of observation, a healthy curiosity, and a cheerful nature – traits that would later stand him in excellent stead as a portrait photographer, who not only needed to have a good eye, but be good with people.

Notman family tradition holds that he was dissuaded from becoming an artist – his first choice of vocation – by his father. Perhaps William Senior's experience with the Paisley shawls had soured him on the idea of indulging in art. In the event, the photographer-to-be became a junior partner in the family dry goods business. Somewhere along the way, he became fascinated with photography and took it up as a hobby. And he must have been a serious amateur, for early photography was a complicated affair, and the man who opened up his first studio in Montreal knew what he was about right from the start.

Around 1955, preparing for the imminent centenary of the establishment of the Notman Studio in Montreal, Notman's youngest son Charles presented the official version of the story of his father's departure from Scotland: "In 1856 he was offered and accepted a position in the Ogilvy dry goods firm of Montreal & came out to Canada."

Indeed, William came to be employed by the firm of Ogilvy & Lewis. But there was a special reason for his coming to Canada when he did and how he did: he was a fugitive from justice, a fact uncovered in the 1970s and 1980s by the McCord Museum's assiduous researchers, Stanley Triggs and Rosina Fontein.

During the 1850s when the Scottish economy suffered a downturn, the Notman dry goods firm became indebted to Marling, Strachan & Co., its major supplier of woollen merchandise in England. When this company cut off the Notmans' credit, stipulating that it would only sell them goods to cover documented orders, the Notmans were deprived of the means by which they might climb out of debt. It was a vicious circle from which the younger William sought to break loose by resorting to what he assumed was a harmless ruse. He ordered double the quantity of material from Marling than he needed, and looked for customers to sell the surplus to – all in the service of paying off his debt to his supplier.

The plan misfired. In June 1856 Notman made a clean breast of his deception to Marling, who took a dim view of it, and turned up in Glasgow accompanied by a bailiff. Caught off guard and cowed by the Englishman, the Notmans signed papers incriminating themselves, and a few days later William Senior was arrested. In the meantime, the two Williams hatched a plan. The father would stay to face the music; the son would make a run for it. According to Scots law, he was "fugitated" – declared a runaway, whose property reverted to the Crown.

The family business quickly collapsed into bankruptcy. Its inventory was seized and all the Notmans' possessions were put up for auction. There was an investigation and trial and William Senior did a short stint in debtors' jail. The blame for the family's disgrace could squarely be placed on the shoulders of the eldest son.

The future photographer was the eldest of seven children. His memories of the idyllic holidays in Kilmun were tinged with nostalgia for childhood jaunts with his brothers and sisters. When he fled, he left behind two sisters (the elder of whom held a strong grudge against him). There were two very young siblings, Maggie and James, age ten and seven respectively at the time of the family disaster, who had to stay with their parents. Brother John, then twenty-six, also remained, presumably as mainstay for the mother.

That left nineteen-year-old Robert, eleven years William's junior. Perhaps he was William's favourite, the one he helped up the rocky ledges when they clambered their way to the Hermit's hut, or sheltered in his arms when the waves rose on the choppy loch, as Duncan the ferryman struggled to bring the sailboat back to shore in a sudden squall. On the eve of departure, when his father urged Notman to get out of Glasgow post haste, Robert might well have begged for a chance to go along, pleaded for the opportunity to help William make a fortune, because as everybody knew there were fortunes to be made in Canada.

In the event he succeeded in accompanying William.

The details of their journey to Canada are lost, save one. William was violently seasick the entire voyage across the Atlantic. They docked in Montreal on August 1, 1856 and were employed almost immediately by Ogilvy & Lewis, whose wholesale dry goods firm stood at the corner of St. Joseph and St. Paul streets. They must have been very busy getting themselves established, since they didn't pick up letters that the newspapers advertised as awaiting them at the post office until September 20, 1856. Almost certainly some of those letters were from William's wife, Alice, to whom he never referred in any other way than "dear Alice," and whom he had married three years earlier.

Alice Woodwark came from the village of Nailsworth, in the district of Stroud, the same part of England that Marling, Strachan & Co., Notman's suppliers, were centred. Stroud was a cloth town with woollen mills powered by the many rivers of the region and supplied by the flocks of sheep grazing on the flanks of the nearby Cotswold hills.

At one time, William Notman had been a travelling salesman for Marling and had probably met Alice in the course of his work. His love for her extended to her parents, and the fondness was reciprocated. Richard Woodwark, Alice's father, held him in enough esteem to keep his letters. The couple's first child, Fanny, was born in Glasgow in July 1855, but when William fled Scotland, Alice and Fanny returned to her parents.

A generation earlier, an uncle of Richard Woodwark had settled on a farm in the Montreal area and had thrived. This may have been one reason why Notman chose the city as his place of refuge. But Montreal in the 1850s was also beginning to hit its stride as Canada's industrial, commercial, and cultural capital. It had a great deal going for it.

By the time the Notman brothers arrived, the city had put behind it the worst ravages of several cholera epidemics and a major fire in 1852, not to mention the disgrace of the burning of the Parliament buildings seven years earlier, which had resulted in its permanent loss of status as the colony's political capital. There was a mood of expansiveness, almost a swagger about the place. A lot of its confidence came from the successful completion of the Grand Trunk Railway, the precursor of the Canadian National system. By 1856 the Grand Trunk reached west to Toronto and Windsor and onward to the border with Michigan, opening up huge markets in the interior for Montreal merchants. The Grand Trunk also ran southeast to the ice-free port of Portland, Maine.

Even though Montreal lies considerably inland, nowadays we regard it as an ocean port. In the mid-nineteenth century, however, ships could only reach the city in the spring, summer, and early fall months, before freeze-up began. The city's entrepreneurial merchants were eager for greater access to outside markets. By achieving a railway connection between Portland, Maine, and Longueuil, Canada East, on the south shore of the St. Lawrence, they brought the railway enticingly close to the south easterly trading partners made available by the Reciprocity Treaty, or free-trade agreement, negotiated with the United States in 1854.

The great obstacle to this commerce was the actual river, two miles of torrential water or ice (and – in spring – great blocks of melting ice or ice shoves), a nightmare to bridge. This monumental engineering challenge was met by the construction of the Victoria Bridge, a railway bridge for which construction began in 1854 and would end six years later. By the time the Notmans arrived the goal of direct access by rail to the city of Montreal on its island, to ice-free water in the Atlantic, was nearly at hand.

At the same time, the Lachine Canal had recently been widened and improved, its four locks overcoming a steep drop of fourteen yards over the course of eight-and-a-half miles from Lac Saint Louis to the Montreal harbour. As the water passed through these locks, factories sprang up alongside. Flour mills, sugar refineries, cotton factories were brand new industries manufacting the goods that until then the city had had to import.

Robert Notman had been right in his night-time discussions and pleadings with his older brother. Fortunes could be made here. And they were being made. The new American magazine *Harpers' Weekly* declared in August 1860: "As a commercial city Montreal has won a high position: It is beyond all question, the first city in British North America." A German visitor observed a year later that "the commercial advantages with which Montreal has been endowed both by nature and art, have called forth a vigorous life in the city at which the traveller is really astonished. At every step you find a building or an institution just begun or just completed... Everything new is constructed on a scale that far exceeds present wants..."

A man could start out with a clean slate in this town and prosper. In addition, a cohesive Scottish community welcomed newcomers. Though Scots numbered only about sixteen per cent of the population, since the days of the fur trade they had been piling up wealth and influence. Between industriousness and general smarts, they had a proverbial finger in every business pie. The Notman brothers were quickly employed by Scotsmen and befriended by Mr. and Mrs. Alexander Ramsay, a hospitable couple with proverbial hearts of gold. By the beginning of November 1856, three scant months after his arrival in Montreal, William had not only sent for Alice and little Fanny, they had already arrived. A free man reunited with his beloved and their cherished child, he was now in a position to home in on his mission. He must make good and bury the sins of the past. He must send for his parents and remaining siblings at the first opportunity. And he must ensure – even if it meant turning night into day – that he would never go bankrupt again.

CHAPTER FIVE

Dear Alice

ALICE NOTMAN HAD A FLAIR for writing, be it letters, recollections, or recipes. What she didn't have was time away from what she called her "duties": being a true helpmate to William, caring for a brood of seven, running a large household without much of a staff, cultivating a social life, and meeting the demands of her strong faith. The incomplete record she has left behind yields the impression of a woman who embodied the positive attributes of Victorian domesticity but was saved from the fate of the long-suffering "angel in the house" by wit and a sense of humour.

Only fragments remain of the steady correspondence with the parents she left behind in England and to whom she was devoted. But her trip to Montreal left a deep impression on her, and she documented it both immediately and twenty years after the fact.

"My very dearest Mamma," she penned on November 6, 1856, two days after her arrival in the city, "I have so much to tell you that I scarcely know how to begin...."

She began with the final stretch of the journey, some 120 miles east of Quebec City, in the vicinity of Rivière-du-Loup, aboard the S.S. *Canadian*, part of the fleet of the Allan Steamship Line owned by the self-same Hugh and Andrew Allan who would hire Dr. Patton as a ship's surgeon. A three-masted clipper, the *Canadian* was a thoroughly modern ship, launched a mere two years earlier, and designed to be powered by both steam and an impressive spread of sails. The *Canadian*'s maiden voyage took only twelve days in September of 1854, and even as late in the season as November, she was likely to make this passage in a fortnight.

Unless of course some disaster befell, such as striking a rock with "a grating thumping noise" at three in the morning. It was, as Alice recalled in a brief memoir in 1878, a "terrible sound once heard never forgotten," the ship "groaning as in mortal agony...." There then followed "a no less terrible silence."

A few hours previously, the ladies' cabin had been the scene of eager enthusiasm: "The Lamp ... shed its dim light on several individuals busily engaged, some intent on adding last lines to letters to be posted on our arrival, writing up journals of the voyage and congratulating each other on its near termination, and some full of bright anticipation of the happy meeting we longed for with those for whose sake we had encountered the perils of the sea and left behind our native land...."

After the initial shock, a candle was lit "and what a group of pale awestruck faces were seen clustering together ... seeking mutual comfort and encouragement." The faces belonged to several young single women and some seven or eight married ladies, all "going out to join their husbands in divers [*sic*] parts of Canada...." Their anxiety was greatly alleviated, however, when Captain Buchanan popped his head into the cabin, beaming reassurance despite a brusque manner. He bade them keep their spirits up and to dress themselves and their children as warmly as possible, to prepare for any eventuality.

The following morning dawned damp and foggy, "& all hands set to work to get the luggage & cargo out of the hold...." A load of iron chains and rails was thrown overboard to lighten the boat and dislodge it from the rock. The great bustle and excitement brought home to the devout Alice the gravity of the situation. "We could not persuade ourselves it was Sunday for there was not a sign of Sabbath rest...." As the day wore on, lowering skies signalled an approaching storm and the prospects of the becalmed *Canadian* turned even grimmer. But then, like a shaft of unexpected sunshine, a small steamer hove into view.

Captain Buchanan ordered the immediate evacuation of the passengers, instructing the women to rush to their staterooms to collect what Alice quaintly called their "personalities" – their toiletries. She was convinced she would never see the rest of her carefully packed trunks again.

Transferred to the little steamer, they and the thirty children with them were assigned cramped and dirty quarters. "Our first agreement was to give up the beds to the invalids and the little children.... I remember laying my little girl by the side of two young Britons, happily quieted by sleep, and their Mother and myself sitting down on the floor beside them to watch their slumber and pass the night as best we could." It would be another eighteen hours before they reached Quebec City. The fare was rough and ready, but "We did not need to be really hungry, as a barrel or two of ship Biscuits were placed on the deck and we could help ourselves."

They passed through customs at Quebec the next morning, and from then on it was smooth sailing. The *John Munn*, a luxury paddle steamer that William had booked for the last leg of their journey, was awaiting in the harbour. On it "we had greater comfort than we had had all the way from England a beautiful Saloon with Piano in it & a fine large Ladies Cabin with a warm stove & nice large berths & lots of the beautiful Canadian apples to feast on...."

At this point, when all was finally well, Alice dropped her cheerful guard. "I felt perfectly worn out too tired to look forward almost & for the first time since I left Liverpool had a good cry I was so done & Fan was so cross...."

She had had a good cry in Liverpool too. That was where she parted with her steady, stiff-upper-lipped father, in his top hat and frock coat, holding rosy-cheeked Fanny in his arms, as they queued up for the boat. Seven miles of interconnected docks stretched along the shore of the Mersey River estuary, so monumental an enterprise that the American author Herman Melville had recently compared it to the construction of the Egyptian pyramids. Countless masts met their eyes in every direction, and pennants in all the colours of the rainbow flapped on the masts. Longshoremen loading and unloading vessels from every conceivable place on earth were also of many hues: black Africans, sallow Irish, dark Malays, golden Asiatics, for this was the Empire's second-largest port.

Mr. Woodwark tried to distract them both from what was uppermost in their minds by asking if Alice knew that some called this place 'the New York of Europe,' for forty per cent of the world's trade passed through Liverpool.

Alice nodded, without hearing a word. Her stomach churned with rising disquiet. Which of the throng of graceful ships, their huge bows festooned with fanciful carvings, was the Canadian? And how would all these vessels manage not to blunder into one another when the moment of departure arrived?

As if reading her thoughts, her father pointed to a clipper, distinct with the red, white, and black funnels of the Allan Line. On its prow, in bold black lettering, was emblazoned the word she both dreaded and anticipated.

The reality of the imminent separation seized Alice so fiercely she could scarcely breathe. With her mother there had already been a wrenching farewell at Nailsworth. Now her father was the last link with all that was dear and familiar. Never to see him again, never to return home as she had done recently! Not that she yearned to do so in the circumstances that had forced her back with little Fanny. A barbed pleasure it had been, taking refuge with her parents. A woman's place was with her husband, not her parents. But in the haste of William's fugitation, there had been no question of accompanying him with a tiny child. The shame of that fugitation! And all because of a small mistake! He had meant no harm, was honest as the day is long. Would he be able to overcome the awful setback he had fled? And what would her life be like in that vast cold place?

At twenty-four, Alice had already weathered a series of dislocations. When she was fourteen, her older brother had died, leaving her suddenly an only child, with all that entailed of devotion and cosseting by her parents. When she married her Scotsman and moved to Glasgow, she moved from a placid rural existence to a noisy, bustling city where even the sound of the Queen's English was foreign.

But by nature she was cheerful and adaptable. If she ever wondered about what fractured American dialect of English she was likely to hear in Montreal, she could take quiet confidence from the fact that she was prepared for the sound and sense of French. Among Alice's prized possessions, packed in her trunk and signed in her neat, slanted hand, was a Bible, acquired on December 13, 1851, when she was nineteen. Though published in London, it was printed in French. As if she had intuited her future in a French city, young Alice Merry Woodwark had either tried to teach herself French or sought to improve on prior knowledge, by studying the text with which she was most intimate.

A ship's horn resounded, and Fanny gave a wail. The sky began to spit, and the drizzle blended with the tears Alice tried unsuccessfully to check. She grabbed Fanny from her father and clung to him for only an instant. Then she turned her back on Liverpool and England and existence as she had so far known it and began to march up the gangplank.

She put the tears away on the boat. The cheerful camaraderie of the ladies' cabin bolstered her spirits and drove home the fact that her plight was far from unique. God would provide. William would be waiting. They would make a new life and also, again with God's help, new lives, sons as well as daughters. The Lord helped those who helped themselves.

On the voyage over she read and reread the letter of Great-Uncle William Woodwark that her father had given her as a kind of talisman. When the ocean pitched and Fan fretted and cried out, Alice recited the letter to her in a soothing voice, skipping over the initial paragraphs where Great-Uncle had written of his daughter's death of fever. Such information was unsuitable for a toddler's ears and frightening even to her own. Instead she paraphrased the information that Great Uncle relayed. ("Listen to this, little Fan. Great-Great-Uncle William brought along all his sheep on the boat to Canada! And they all arrived hale and hearty.") And when Fan slept she reread the details of the smooth transition Great-Uncle had made from the Old World to the new, with almost the focus she gave the Good Book.

The letter was dated Lachine, July 31, 1831, having been written a year before Alice was born. Addressed to "Dear Nephew and Niece," it was intended for Alice's parents. It spoke of a friendly and open society, of meeting a British butcher on the steamboat from Quebec to Montreal "who had been at Montreal for some years, he took us and our luggage to his house, we stayed with him a week, and he introduced us to many respectable English and Scotch farmers, and they said that I should have a farm upon the Island of Montreal, for it was preferable to the Upper Canada … for the markets are so much better." Indeed, Great-Uncle went on to purchase fifty-five acres in Lachine, "a healthful pleasant village … nine miles from Montreal at the head of the canal that goes to the Upper Country." The property included a four-storey stone farmhouse, with six rooms per floor and a total of thirty-five glass windows! He spoke of the bounty of the land in the vernacular of farmers: "Vegetation is wonderfully rapid in this country as wheat is not more than 14 or 15 weeks from sowing to reaping; great breadths of potatoes are planted here, many farmers have 20 or 30 acres and some more, the land is of blackest soil and grow[s] abundant crops…. There are a great many hops grown in this country, pumpkins are planted among the Indian Corn which grow to a large size, here are the fruitfulest gardens I ever saw, there are a great many onions grown here which are shipped to other Countries, plenty of cucumbers, melons and grapes and all kinds of fruit, the grapes wild in the woods." Despite the death of the daughter with which the letter began, it exuded enthusiasm. "We are all satisfied with our new situation, the dwelling house fronts the river which leads to Quebec, and there is a beautiful little Indian village across the river called Cocanuogan, there is nothing but Indians upon it."

All this was well and good for a farmer, but Alice's Willie was a dry goods merchants and salesman, with an artistic bent and a hankering for photography. Great-Uncle William's effusions however were still applicable to the urban members of his extended family. "Montreal is a very flourishing City, they are building wharf and stores for the convenience of shipping and they are building large stores and dwelling houses in all parts of the town, all built of stone. Two new Steamboats were launched last week. There is a market for every day in the week for butchers meat and all kinds of vegetables and fowls and numbers of carts standing the market with lambs, calves, pigs and all kinds of grain." Again and again he referred to prosperity. "I have met with a great many friends both English and Scotch farmers who have been here for some years and are doing very well."

Alice must have silently congratulated herself for her efforts in improving her French. Great Uncle sent a message in the letter for one Joseph Wood back home who "might do very well if he was here… and if he could speak the French language before he came it would be an advantage to him."

The *John Munn* docked in Montreal on November 4, 1856 at eight o'clock in the morning in a dense fog that did not impede her progress, for, "in about 10 minutes," Alice wrote her mother, "I once more saw with feelings of inexpressible joy & thankfulness my beloved Husband and felt that I was all right." They had been apart almost five months and the reunion was marked by tears and laughter and a sense of great relief. "You can imagine but I cannot describe our feelings and how delighted he was with his child – so much grown & improved." William quickly collected the luggage that, despite Alice's worries, was intact, and "he soon had us in a Cab ... & we were rattling through the streets of Montreal & very strange & unreal it seemed."

The generosity and hospitality of Canadians that Great-Uncle William Woodwark had been so struck by a generation earlier held true in the case of the Notmans. Mr. and Mrs. Alexander Ramsay, William's new friends, had advised him not to take lodgings in a boarding house, as it would cost too much. William, wrote Alice, "told me that our more than kind friends the Ramsays would take no denial to their invitation from me to go there till *our house* was ready & so we drove there and dear Mrs R received me as if I had been a dear sister & made me feel completely at home in a few minutes."

The house at 147 St. Antoine Street was a large establishment, "well furnished & everything in good order." Oil and colour merchant Alexander Ramsay's shop at the corner of St. James and McGill streets claimed to be the oldest paint company in Canada and was clearly a going concern. The Ramsays had a son of sixteen still at home, along with Mrs. Ramsay's father ("a very nice old man"), and Jeanie, her niece ("a real kind nice girl), and a certain Mr. Mitchell "who boards with them out of kindness on their part because his wife took to evil ways & left him & he was so miserable & lonely that Mrs R could not bear not to have him in the house to cheer him up a little."

Mr. and Mrs. Ramsay, Alice later commented, themselves knew what it was to be strangers in a strange land. Out of this empathy was born their benevolence. Alice found herself "in a most comfortable bedroom with every comfort as I had it at home...." Only a couple of days after her arrival, she was already used to going to the cupboards to get whatever she needed. "And you can't think how they all love Fanny ... They seem to take as great an interest in all our concerns – As if they were the nearest relatives – I can only feel that it is God who has so warmed their hearts to us...."

The Notmans lived with the Ramsays for three weeks until their own small house was ready to receive them. Their initiation into Canadian ways began on St. Antoine Street, and Alice took to the new life with relish. "They keep no servant & everyone helps the other & you don't know how well everything goes on." Years later she expanded on the subject of do-it-yourself homemaking, commenting that *chez* Ramsay she humbly learned some incalculably useful lessons. "The self help we saw all around was in a great degree a novel experience – people doing their own work and not beginning to try to do it sub-rosa, but with a comfortable content that it was well done as no one could do it for you." It was both surprising and pleasing "to see the head of the house going to market and carrying home a basket of provisions as a matter of course." Even young ladies of that time, Alice observed with gentle irony "felt able to carry home a pair of gloves or a necktie."

The New World was a great social leveller. "I was struck," she wrote in 1878, "by the air of perfect equality in the working classes, so different from what one was used to. I remember the odd feeling when I heard a butterwoman ask at the door if the woman of the house needed anything." (It gave Alice – reared in class-conscious England – a jolt to be referred to as a "woman" rather than a "lady.") She also recalled being "rather quenched by the way an old Irishman at work in the cellar accepted a bowl of tea as if he took it to oblige me."

The plenty and comfort of Canadian domestic life hugely impressed her. "Everything seemed in such abundance, such piles of lovely apples, such large dishes of honey and preserves, such variety of pies, such nice tea four times a day." She contrasted the wafer-thin bread and butter of English tea time with "good thick honest slices fit for hungry people. Oh how good it all tasted, and the hearty welcome with it made it doubly sweet."

Like all newcomers to Canada she was daunted by her first Canadian winter, which that year was particularly severe and set in early. As she scrutinized the elaborate preparations being made for the change of seasons in the Ramsay household, "I own to feeling in my heart a little dismayed at the prospect, thinking it must be something terrible if these precautions I saw going on around me were really necessary." Not only were double windows being installed but "every little crevice by which the fresh air could enter" was stuffed with rags. The snow that blanketed the city even before the official advent of winter "seemed so strange. ... I could scarce believe we were to see these strange looking wooden pavements no more till the Spring."

The Notman family moved to their own place at 11 Bleury Street on December 1. They arrived by sleigh, taking "the merry tinkle of the bells" as an omen of welcome to their new Canadian home. It was a small red brick house – possibly once an old farmhouse – destined to double both as private home and the first Notman photographic studio. There were so few dwellings along this stretch of Bleury from St. Catherine to Sherbrooke that to walk along it at night was, according to Alice "dismal." The nights were also made fearsome by the frequent knolling of a "terrible bell" at the nearby fire station at the corner of Bleury and Craig streets.

Another surviving letter from Alice to her parents picks up the story of the Notmans' lives four weeks after their move. Writing on a Sunday between Christmas and New Year's, Alice sounded pensive and wistful. "Oh dear dear Mamma & Papa I wonder how you are this bleak looking Sabbath day – and how you spent Christmas. ... We spent Christmas day at the Ramsays & had plum pudding & mince pie quite in an orthodox manner & had a very pleasant day. They had some friends to tea & We had some music in the evening & were very happy & came home in a sleigh with Fanny under the Buffaloe [sic] skins singing all the way home. My thoughts were often over the sea and memory was busy with old times and many a wish was wafted across the Atlantic that now rolls between us – do you know I find it very hard to realize that I am really in Canada & I do not feel one quarter as far from England as I know you do from us...."

It is in this letter that the first surviving references to William's future career are planted, but in the way Alice alludes to them it seems likely that her parents already were familiar with these ambitions. "Dear William has his photographing plan ready – and I think will be doing some business in that line next week. He works early & late at it & seems to have a chance of success." Alice reported that

William had secured an order "from Mr Lewis one of his employers to take the likenesses of his family. He told W. he thought it a first rate thing to employ his spare time & told him he was at liberty to take any time he might require 'till the busy season begins again."

Towards the end of the letter Alice reverted to the subject of photography, in the context of news from William's family in Glasgow. She had a series of complaints against her in-laws. "They were still uncertain about the [legal] case but seemed to hope rather than fear.... They expect to hear [from us] every week, but we think once a fortnight plenty, don't you? They are always fault finding with my dear Husband.... Jessie [one of William's sisters] wrote what I considered a most impertinent letter of advice to her brother & they refused to help him by sending out some things he required for Photographing. It will be very long before he asks anything again, but wait awhile if God enables him to get on, the tide will soon turn.... To see my darling husband unjustly thought of & treated as if he were a child without a particle of common sense or judgement..., but it will all work round in time."

Even accounting for the normal friction between a daughter-in-law and her husband's family, there was a tone of special grievance as Alice poured out her heart to her parents. Apparently the Notmans in Glasgow were embittered about William. He, after all, had got away, while they were still mired in the consequences of his errors.

There were a couple of references to brother Robert, who, it appears, was living with them at Bleury Street. "Do you think it is too much for Robert out of a salary of 110 [dollars] to pay [us] for board washing & mending...? I believe they think it – but we dont care – do not mention this to anyone – I only tell you to relieve my mind...."

The brothers were spending a great deal of time together. Robert also was employed by Ogilvy & Lewis, and would subsequently work at photography. Like Alice and William, he appeared to have a strong religious bent, at least as far as attendance at church was concerned. "I never felt the Sabbath more precious than now as a rest to both body & mind, which by the end of the week need a little refreshment. William & Robert were out this morning & heard a good sermon from our good minister & Robert has been at the Sunday School this afternoon." At the age of nineteen, Robert must have been a Sunday school teacher, not a scholar.

Alice said that she herself didn't get much of a chance to get out because of her busy life, but hoped to go to church that evening. As soon as they could afford it, she planned to send out the washing, which was the only part of her duties that she found onerous "but dollars are not very plenty & of course I must save all I can & my beloved is so helpful & handy & never minds doing anything that can save his wife trouble – and oh it is very sweet to work for those we love." Willie had recently secured half a cask of "beautiful" butter at an advantageous price, and they still had some meat left from what he had bought at the market a month earlier "& I have the hardest work to chop any off it, it is as hard as stone…." Despite the extreme cold, the house was warm and cosy and her oven was "the greatest comfort – it bakes so well – I hardly ever buy more than a loaf a week & bake all the rest myself sometimes with baking powder, & at others with yeast made from hops – & it is really very excellent bread – I wish I could send you some."

The Ramsays continued to loom large in their lives, with Mrs. Ramsay calling on Alice once or twice a week and taking "a truly Motherly interest in our welfare," and Mr. Ramsay visiting Willie even more often. So important indeed were they to the Notmans that Alice, a doctrinaire Anglican who believed in Jesus as "the Author & furnisher of our faith," feared for their immortal souls. The Ramsays were Unitarians, acknowledging Jesus only as the "Son of God & the one only mediator but *not equal* in power & glory [to God]…." However, the Notmans and Ramsays steered clear of religious discussion, "but each keep our own views."

It was, no doubt, easier to talk with the Ramsays about more mundane matters, such as the ushering in of 1857. "New Years day is a great day here. *All* the gentlemen pay their respects to the Ladies who stay at home to receive them. Mrs Ramsay had 140 visitors last New Years day – I do not expect to have many." Alice's reflections on the approaching festivities were tinged with melancholy. "When you receive this my dearest Mamma we shall have begun a New Year – and this one which has been so eventful so full of bitter experiences – of hopes &

fears – partings & meetings will have floated away down the River of time and we shall see it no more." She asked for even the most trifling news from home, filled her parents in with details of Fanny's "many little enticing ways," and reassured them of her belief that even if they didn't meet again in this world, they would do so in the next. Yet in another breath she asked God to bless both her parents and little Fanny and expressed the fervent hope that she would yet "have the delight of presenting her once more to you."

It had indeed been a year of turmoil, change, and renewal for Alice and William and by extension for that younger brother – Robert – who was such a model churchgoer in 1856. They were on the cusp of even greater changes.

CHAPTER SIX

The Well-known Photographer

1856-1868

No FEWER THAN SEVEN photography studios lined Buchanan Street, the street where the Notman dry goods business was located in Glasgow. One of them belonged to a Steven Young, who advertised teaching photography "in a few easy lessons." Young also boasted a multitude of choices "in all kinds of Photography, Daguerrotype on Plate, Collodion on Glass, and Talbotype on Paper." Whether William Notman learned from Young or another practitioner, he dabbled early in all these forms. But by all indications, in Scotland he remained a hobbyist.

Montreal gave him the opportunity to recreate himself as a professional. The city had its own photographers by 1856, the dean of whom was T.C. Doane. Billing himself a "Photographist and Daguerrotypist," Doane was, according to Alice Notman, "the principal artist here – but whose productions are very far below W's." She said that Doane had begun his business eight years earlier "with nothing" and was now wishing to retire from his studio at Place d'Armes "with plenty of means."

Here was an incipient opening for Notman. He seized it. A letter he wrote to Alice's father in England in February 1857 reveals an optimistic, lively man, doting on his family, trying to better himself and rectify his past mistakes.

> My dear Sir,
> Many thanks for your more than kind note of Jany 18th....
> God has given us a large measure of health & crowned us with many blessings & the future promises well & I begin to hope I may yet be able to repair at least a part of the loss I was the cause of. Dear Alice would no doubt inform you that I saw fit to give up my situation & bid adieu at least for

a time to the cloths & am now a photographer. I have been giving the subject much attention & expect it will yield me a fair return for my trouble....Our precious little daughter is so loving & pretty[,] full of fun & mischief & a decided taste for pictures which she handles rather roughly when she gets a chance but you could not possibly be *very* angry with her she is so conciliating.

A century later, Notman's youngest son, Charles, set down for posterity the genesis of his father's business as he had heard it from William himself. Ogilvy & Lewis did brisk business during the summer months when the port was open to navigation. But once winter approached there was so little action the staff sat around the stove, whiling the hours away with card games. Notman twitched with impatience and nervous energy at this waste of his time. "He told Mr. Ogilvy that he would like to try his hand at photography," recalled Charles Notman. Were he to fail, he asked to be taken back.

After only a few months' acquaintance, Notman had so impressed his bosses that they not only granted him the requested leave, but offered him a loan with which to purchase the expensive equipment needed to set himself up.

At the back of his little house on Bleury Street he built a room with a skylight and began with portraiture. Customers trooped in right away. "Dear Willie is very busy," Alice wrote in April 1857. "His connexion seems extending. He has been very successful with his Calotypes and seems gradually getting into that business which has always been his wish. Competent judges tell him his prints are the best that have been done in Canada. He has taken Mr Fraser the Free Church Minister ... in his gown & his hand on an open Bible. It is wonderful how much he has had to do – but Photography is a good trade here...."

Alice was working alongside her husband, acting as his receptionist. "While William was out for about an hour & half yesterday afternoon I had to receive 13 people, answer questions & show specimens," she wrote her mother. He was teaching photography as well, "anything to turn a[n] honest penny.... I think it wd do us good to go to bed at 10 for a week, but there are many things he can do only at night where he has no interruption...."

Capturing and freezing an image has grown so ubiquitous and ridiculously simple in our day – the push of a single button – that it is hard to imagine its early complicated technology and initial revolutionary impact. But Notman was tapping into a new art/science that was on the verge of becoming a huge phenomenon. Photography drew on the Victorians' insatiable appetite for collecting; it indulged the new bourgeoisie's cult of the self. It was born in France in 1826 – quite coincidentally the year of Notman's birth – when an inventor called Joseph Nicéphore Niépce produced the earliest surviving photograph of a scene from nature. A view of Niépce's garden taken from his windowsill using a mechanical and optical device called a *camera obscura*, it was titled "Vue de la fenêtre du Gras." Clearly experimental rather than practical, the picture took a whopping eight hours to expose.

Other pioneers of the same period included Louis Daguerre, a sometime partner of Niépce, who invented the daguerreotype process in France, and William Henry Fox Talbot, the British originator of the calotype process.

The idea of fixing an image – arresting time – was what fascinated and obsessed all these innovators: how to document reality exactly and relatively rapidly without drawing or painting, without the mediation of an artist. Louis Daguerre found a way to do it by coating a thin sheet of copper plate with silver, then exposing it to mercury vapour, which he then exposed to light. The resulting extremely fine and detailed image – which took a mere(!) hour to produce – was a direct positive made in the camera. Depending on the angle from which it was viewed and the colour of the surface reflected into it, it changed from positive to negative, producing an ethereal, almost hypnotic effect, as if the viewer were catching the eye of the subject in the ornate little case that held the likeness. While initially popular, daguerrotypes had limited profitability since they were one-of-a-kind artifacts that could not be readily reproduced. A modern, much less romantic or beautiful parallel is the Polaroid snapshot.

Talbot's invention, the calotype, followed Daguerre's by a couple of years. It made use of a negative-positive method using paper instead of a metal plate inside the camera. Like film – its later descendant – the calotype had the great advantage of allowing prints to be made of the original. However, it didn't catch on because the image taken from a paper negative lacked sharpness and precision.

Notman's preferred method came to be wet plate photography. Invented by Frederick Scott Archer in 1851 it was called the "collodion method" and combined the best of Daguerre's and Talbot's systems: it created a sharp and clear image with the capacity for endless replication of prints. This finally enabled photography to become profitable, but at a cost, for wet plate photography was a devilishly difficult art.

The scenario went something like this: A glass negative – or plate – was coated with iodized collodion, a viscous substance, which was made light sensitive by submersion in a silver nitrate bath. Once the photographer was satisfied with his subject's stance and expression, he had to dash from the so-called operating room to the darkroom, coat his plate, run to the camera, insert the plate, expose the picture, and then run back to the darkroom and develop the shot before the chemicals dried.

"From the very start sittings were made of all the prominent families & personages in Montreal," Charles Notman tells us of his father's early career. Details of these first sittings are few, but after William began keeping the glass negatives from which reprints could be made and created a recording system, the scope of his undertakings becomes apparent.

He attracted a large clientele both because his photos were excellent and because he was so good with people. A perfectionist, he took great pains posing his subjects and aiming light in the studio in ways designed to play up their features. He arranged elaborate posing stands to immobilize clients' heads and limbs, so they could relax during the long exposures. And even as he rushed between studio and darkroom, he conveyed an air of calm, resorting to small stratagems to keep customers similarly tranquil.

In the mid 1860s he published a little booklet of advice that is still relevant for a trip to the studio. It was titled *Photography. Things You Ought to Know.* "The one thing needful of a sitter to learn is how to forget himself. If he could be perfectly free from self-consciousness, he would secure a natural and truthful picture.

The operator having a trained eye and long experience, can best determine the most graceful pose, and having his own reputation at stake this may safely be left to his care. ... While a pleasing expression is desirable a characteristic one is still more so, as nothing is so silly or undignified as a forced smile."

Notman became expert at photographing children, a challenge even for those practising photography under much less stressful conditions in a later day. He seems to have had a natural affinity for children and, as his own family expanded, he knew what worked and what didn't. "Avoid giving or mentioning sweets to them. Do not play or fuss too much with them. Generally a child will sit best if left entirely to the operator." One of his favourite gambits to beguile little ones was to caper around the studio with a stuffed lamb on top of his head.

And yet even with his pleasant manners, painstaking attention to craft, and sound sense, William Notman might merely have ended up one of a number of good photographers working in mid-nineteenth century Montreal. There were other fine practitioners in the city. Arguably at least one of them – Alexander Henderson – was a better, more atmospheric artist. But Notman wasn't only an outstanding photographer. He was also an extremely astute businessman.

Shortly after starting out in his new profession, he secured a commission from the Grand Trunk Railway Company to photograph the last stages of the construction of the Victoria Bridge. And then to top this coup, he managed to attract royal attention to his work.

The construction of the bridge involved a colossal feat of engineering. The problem of actual distance was compounded by the surge of ice in early spring when the ice cover broke up. But the goal of direct access by rail from the island of Montreal to ice-free water in the Atlantic was a powerful incentive, and the difficulties were overcome with a sophisticated tubular design: a steel box laid on top of twenty-four cut-stone pediments set into the river. It took five years to build, involved the labour of more than 3,000 men (and many children), and, on completion, became the longest bridge in the world.

How did Notman secure the commission to photograph the Eighth Wonder of the World – as the bridge was known for a time –

in 1858? No one knows for sure. He had obviously demonstrated his skills rapidly and effectively to Montrealers. But for a new immigrant to so thoroughly win over powerful and influential people in his adoptive city was unusual if not unprecedented. With vision, technical expertise, business smarts wedded to charisma and charm, William Notman must have been something of a force of nature.

It's tempting to suggest that photographing the construction of the bridge was as challenging as building it. By this time Notman was working with wet plate photography and glass negatives. For two years – using an eighteen by twenty-two-inch camera in which the plates were the size of window panes – he documented the erection of the bridge. In the days before enlargements were possible, he took mammoth-sized photos, often while balancing precariously at the top of the site. He must have brought along a portable darkroom, because the technology demanded that negatives be coated and sensitized, just as in a studio. The speed necessary for all of this activity required dexterity and sangfroid. His feat remains one of the great achievements of documenting engineering projects, in any age.

He probably had an assistant with him, quite likely his brother Robert, who also worked as a photographer, and who – some ten years later – would be commended under nightmarish circumstances "for the zealous and intelligent assistance" he had rendered his brother "in bringing to the highest possible perfection... the most beautiful art of the age."

Queen Victoria declined an invitation to inaugurate the bridge named after her, but in the summer of 1860 she sent as her proxy the Prince of Wales. The future Edward VII – his career as bon vivant and philanderer still ahead of him – was then a boy of eighteen. The city feted him with balls, galas, and a rather smoky train ride in the tubular engineering marvel. An official memento acknowledging the royal favour was deemed appropriate: the Prince must take back a present for the Queen.

Notman offered up his talents. Victoria was known to be interested in photography: how about a magnificent commemorative album housed in a beautiful box? He prepared a collection of photographs and stereographs of the bridge, along with views of the Canadian landscape and cities. The assortment included "ten of the largest sized plates yet taken in Canada": outsized vistas of the bridge, along with pictures of Niagara Falls, Quebec City, and Montreal. The full set was presented to the prince in two leather-bound portfolios packaged in an attractive box made of Canadian bird's-eye maple.

Repeatedly throughout his career Notman would prove a genius at marketing himself and his work. He had one great idea after another. But for sheer brilliance of imagination, none of his later schemes beats that of the first: the Maple Box. In due course it and its contents arrived in England, where it received good press in the *Illustrated London News* – some five years after its creator had been fugitated from the British Isles. Notman cannily prepared a duplicate set of photos in identical portfolios and decorative box. This remained in Montreal for display in his new studio, a spacious and elegant greystone next door to the humble original. The photographs that had won the favour of the Queen were there for all his customers to admire, a brilliant publicity vehicle showcasing his work and renown.

There are no records to substantiate why, soon after the Maple Box arrived in England, Notman built a portico over the entrance to the studio, its pediment bearing the sign "Photographer to the Queen." Very few photographers were distinguished with such official marks of patronage, but Notman family tradition maintains that the title was indeed bestowed on him by Victoria. Certainly members of the British royal family who visited Montreal in subsequent years all put in appearances at the studio. And the general snob appeal was irresistible: those who possessed the means were fond of being strategically posed astride a horse or in a carriage beneath the famous sign.

By 1860 Notman was stretched too thin to manage the studio with only Alice's help. He began to hire apprentices, photographers, and support staff in the darkroom and finishing rooms. In order to expand his services he created an Art Department, headed by a recent immigrant from England, the talented watercolourist John Arthur Fraser. Under Fraser, several of the city's artists worked at retouching negatives, painting backdrops, colourizing photographs, and eventually producing the huge and complex composite photographs for which Notman's studio became famous.

Over the years thousands of customers crossed the threshold of the imposing double duplex at the foot of Bleury Street. An advantageous location, close to but not directly at the heart of the city – at the time along St. James and Notre Dame streets – it was easy to access both on foot and by carriage. The limestone mansion eventually became headquarters of a photographic empire with branches across Canada and the United States – the largest and most successful such business in North America. Its founder became the first Canadian photographer to earn an international reputation.

On arrival, prospective clients made their way to the reception room. Its majestic dimensions – seventy-five feet long by thirty-five feet wide – took up almost the whole depth of the building. Dozens of enormous photographs and paintings in gilded frames lined the walls, creating an atmosphere of opulence. A visitor related his impressions in 1864: "the walls are completely covered with the finest specimens of the [photographic] art, comprising portraits of celebrities, foreign and local, many of which are exquisitely finished in water colours and oil; here will also be found some very fine paintings …. with many choice proof engravings which give diversity and add interest of the whole." As a direct result of the interplay between photographer and artists, Notman's magnificent reception room came to be used for art exhibitions, the only venue in the city with the cachet of an art gallery, the precursor of the Montreal Museum of Fine Arts.

Behind a large L-shaped counter in a corner of the room, a receptionist greeted customers, distributed finished photographs, and supplied a fount of pertinent information about sessions with "the operator." Receptionists were usually women. (By the early 1870s a third of Notman's fifty-odd employees were female.) These "greeters" might provide a selection of catalogues which clients leafed through in search of a painted backdrop created by members of the Art Department to suit a variety of tastes.

Photography consciously patterned itself on the conventions of painting, where an artist would paint an evocative background for his model. Thus Notman's subjects could choose to be depicted through a kind of *trompe l'oeil*, in a palatial home, in a pretty garden, or out in the countryside. Backdrops were meant to give context to a photograph and to create mood. Sometimes they featured a classical ornament, such as a column or balustrade – objects symbolic of wealth and grandeur. In other pictures the backdrop was bucolic – perhaps a quaint bridge straddling a stream in the shade of a leafy tree.

The receptionist also dispensed advice about apparel suitable for the sitting. She might sell a copy of, or refer to, Notman's booklet of very precise do's-and-don'ts. For instance, the photographer valued a lace scarf or an "opera mantle" for enhancing a lady's grace, but insisted on restraint in her coiffure: "avoid dressing the hair in any style unusual to the individual, or wearing any unfamiliar kind of head dress."

Notman added that "Uniforms, fancy dresses, and articles of ladies' attire" could be sent ahead to the studio, "where dressing rooms are provided for the use of visitors." Female members of the staff would be able to assist ladies with their toilette in the changing rooms.

Notman was a good, unflappable employer, who held on to his staff even in economic downturns. Summary firings occurred only for egregious offences, as when a Peeping Tom drilled a little hole in the wall of the ladies' changing room. (In a later era, Notman's son, Charles, fired a man on the spot for taking a picture of one of the female staff in the washroom with her breasts exposed. Charles discovered the negatives in the darkroom.) And there was no reprieve for one John Kerr, who dropped and shattered the best negative of photos taken of Prince Arthur in December 1869.

A great deal of the studio's bread and butter was earned from shots of the British soldiers garrisoned in Montreal, for protection against the risk of Fenian invasion from the United States. The officers adored being portrayed in wintry scenes done up in the studio, where, garbed in their uniforms, they sported snowshoes or pirouetted on fake ice.

Charles Notman later recalled a couple of great soldier anecdotes. "One day a young officer of the Rifle Brigades came in to cancel his appointment for a sitting as he had a black eye. So Father took him up to the Artist room & had his eye painted so it did not show. And after that every few days a young blade would come in to have his eye painted & so many came in that father decided to charge $5.00 & still they came."

And then there was the hoity-toity officer who complained about the quality of his colourized portrait. Such pictures took a great deal of work by an artist, but Notman still agreed to redo the portrait. When the customer remained displeased with the result, Notman drew the line, and asserted that the portrait was a fine likeness. Upon this "the officer handed out a $20.00 bill in payment & tore the picture up & threw it on the counter & my father immediately tore the $20.00 bill up. The officer [then] smiled & shook hands & was a very good customer from then on."

Domestically, too, the early years in Montreal were an expansive and happy time for the Notman family. In the summer of 1858 William wrote to his English in-laws so far away across the ocean, "I wish you … could look in sometimes & see us, it would not take long to see that we were a happy circle… and I thank God that he has so blessed and prospered me here that we can send from time to time such cheering accounts of the health and happiness of dear Alice and our two Sweetest treasures." Little Willie, the couple's first Canadian-born child, was a sickly baby, his health causing much anxiety, but, wrote William "it has pleased God to partially restore his health." When part of the home studio was destroyed by fire, luckily there was some insurance, and most fortunately "Alice & the wee ones were not staying there."

By 1859, Notman had brought out his parents, his adult brother John, and the two youngest siblings, Maggie and James, from Scotland. An 1859 stereograph of the extended family shows a pregnant Alice seated in the front row, her head supported by the crook of William's arm as he stands behind her. Little Fanny sits front and centre between her grandparents, while little Willie is ensconced in William Senior's lap. In the back row, posed directly behind his parents, stands a younger, equally handsome version of the photographer William: tall, high-browed, even featured Robert.

The family continued to grow: three little girls were born to Alice between 1859 and 1865. When she and William buried a stillborn son in February 1862, an unquestioning religious faith carried them through their loss. In one of his letters, William wrote his father-in-law, "Godsways [sic] are not as our ways." In another, there's a note of resignation and acceptance: "we must leave it in his hands who ordereth all things wisely & well."

Piety and orthodoxy didn't interfere with Notman's love of the good things of life, and he clearly enjoyed acquiring marks of wealth as he thrived. In the mid-1860s the family moved to 34 Berri Street, a row house in a brand new residential neighbourhood off Viger Square. Early in January 1864, he shared some exciting news with his in-laws. "Dear Alice has told you of my having bought 'Clyde-side,' for a summer residence." A gingerbread cottage festooned with roses on Lower Lachine Road, Clydeside was a lovely spot on the St. Lawrence. The Notman family installed themselves there in full comfort; their fourth daughter, Emily, was born in the summer house in August 1865.

Notman campaigned hard for Alice's parents to immigrate to Canada, as his own family had done, and he encouraged them to overlook the rigours of the climate. At the same time he did a little gentle boasting. "I do not think you need to be afraid of our winters. No doubt we have it sometimes very cold, but then all our arrangements are made for it & you would be surprised how pleasant it is both out & in…. This winter … I propose driving out more, having bought a nice horse and sleigh. So you may expect to hear of dear Alice and our darlings taking sundry short trips."

He took a keen interest in the political changes afoot in his adoptive land. In September 1864 leading politicians from Nova Scotia, New Brunswick, Prince Edward Island and the two Canadas met in Charlottetown to discuss the possibility of union among the Maritime and Canadian colonies. In October, a two-week long conference in Quebec City followed on the heels of Charlottetown. "You will see by the papers," Notman wrote in November 1864, "that at present there is a movement to unite the provinces in this quarter under one government. I hope whatever may be the issue that it will prove a benefit to the country. We have had the principal visitors with us to be photographed & so far as the movement has gone it has been one of profit to me." John A. Macdonald, Thomas

D'Arcy McGee, George Brown, George-Étienne Cartier, Hector Langevin, Charles Tupper, and Samuel Leonard Tilley all visited the studio in the mid-1860s; in the years to come so would most of the other Fathers of Confederation.

The scent of budding nationhood also inspired Notman to look for ideas in the bosom of his family. During the first week of January 1867, he featured his nine-year-old son, William McFarlane Notman, in a winter portrait entitled "Young Canada." Growing up in the studio and destined to become a fine photographer in his own right, Willie Notman had been his father's model from infancy. Many photographs of the little boy were created not merely for family consumption, but for sale to the general public as souvenirs or collectors' items. In "The Newsboy," taken in 1866, Willie played the part of a weather-toughened newsie, a sheaf of newsprint under one arm, as he held his hood closed with a mittened fist against a blinding blizzard. But in "Young Canada," he was a wide-eyed innocent (like a younger, more privileged brother of the newsboy) perched on a pile of rocks under a couple of straggly trees. Height of fashion, he was bundled up in a little Red River coat, belted with a wide sash, a scarf dusted with snow wrapped around his neck. Had the picture been colourized, it would have shown a coat of navy blue worsted with scarlet piping that matched the shade of the sash. A toque beneath his hood, high leggings over his breeches and snowshoes strapped to his feet completed Willie's outfit. In the foreground, snow adorned the rocks and clung to the trunks and branches of the trees. Snowflakes streamed from the sky and landed on Willie's cheek, the snowy studio backdrop blending seamlessly with the field of snow in which the rocks – cunningly sprinkled with white rock salt – were arranged. For of course all this was a composition created indoors.

The timing of the photograph merged flawlessly with new political realities. For just as Notman was splattering his negative with white paint in the early days of 1867, in London delegates from the colonies that would band together in the new Dominion on July 1, were hammering out the provisions of the British North America Act to which the Queen gave royal assent on March 29. The picture would sell as a kind of genre portrait of an ingénue country, a photo not so much of Willie as a child, but of a wintry nation at the dawn of birth.

By the mid-1860s Notman had won a couple of medals at international exhibitions in London and Paris, and celebrities from around the world flocked to his door. Among the first was Henry Wadsworth Longfellow, the most renowned American poet of his day, who arrived in 1862. In the same year, Notman posed the diminutive Harriet Beecher Stowe seated at a carved table equipped with a writing tablet, books, a keepsake box, and a vase of flowers. The author of the abolitionist novel *Uncle Tom's Cabin* had a fondness for Montreal. Returning to the city in 1869, she was much taken by its "mountain of churches" and spent a Sunday touring as many as she could fit in. Henry Ward Beecher, Harriet's younger brother, was the most charismatic and famous preacher of his time. Notman photographed him in 1867, a few years before the notorious adultery trial airing his relationship with a married woman.

In 1867 Notman shot a long domestic series of the family of Jefferson Davis, the former President of the Confederate States during the American Civil War. This was a couple of years after Davis's wife and large family took refuge in Montreal, while Davis was locked away in a federal prison in Virginia.

The Confederacy enjoyed great popularity with upscale Montrealers, not because slavery was especially appealing as a cause but because of a general suspicion of Yankee intent to annex British North America, and admiration for the gracious manners of the many vacationing Southerners who frequented Montreal to escape their steamy summer clime.

The hosts of the refugee Davises were the printer and publisher John Lovell and his erudite wife, Sarah. As Mrs. Lovell wrote in a memoir, "We could not but sympathize with the Southerners in the loss of their luxurious homes, and of many near and dear to them." Whether William Notman thought of Davis and family other than as celebrity cash cows is not evident. But many years after they were gone from Montreal, a family pet sported the name "Jefferson Davis."

And then there suddenly came an event that stemmed the flow of all that was bountiful and happy in the remade life of William

Notman. On June 2, 1867, one month before the new Dominion was declared, Fanny Notman – that delightful little girl upon whom her parents had doted, the precious toddler with whom her father could not be angry, even when she ripped apart his photos – died of meningitis at the age of eleven.

It was an era in which such occurrences were common, when infectious disease could decimate a family. The trappings of mourning were many: the laying-out of the corpse in the front parlour, the black armband, the widow's weeds. One of the lesser-known appurtenances of mourning was the custom of taking pictures of the dead, a service Notman advertised and practised although not of his own kin.

Did the family rally around Alice, William and the four remaining children? Were pieties uttered about the world to come? By this time the Woodwarks, Alice's parents whom William had finally enticed to immigrate, were living in Montreal, and so the gleanings about the private Notman can no longer be harvested.

Around this time of domestic tragedy, Notman's younger brother Robert began acting out. Again.

CHAPTER SEVEN

The Sunday School Teacher

March, 1868

ANGRY QUESTIONS SWARM *like the drone of wasps in Robert Notman's head as he lies rigid on his pallet in a holding cell on the first floor of the Pied-du-Courant Gaol.*

What had possessed that fool Alfred Patton to swallow poison?

How could a doctor not notice that Mag had the constitution of a draft mare? (He – Robert – had repeatedly dosed her with enough potions to abort a dozen girls. With no effect whatsoever.)

Why, oh why, had poor Alfred not waited for the morning? Did not the Psalmist say, "Weeping may tarry for the night, But joy cometh in the morning"? And did not Mag rally, as Robert had known all along she would?

If not for the doctor's crazed impulse, no one today would suspect a thing. Well, perhaps, the hotelier…. That Mr. Hogan possessed a most piercing gaze, and with every glance and word he had communicated the message that he wasn't to be hoodwinked. But Robert was footing the bill, and an innkeeper trades in discretion. No harm would have come to anyone. Not to Alfred and not to Robert. And even Mag was now recovering nicely, according to rumour. At the General Hospital on Dorchester Street.

But for all the buzzing of his circular thoughts Robert is at heart an optimist. As the wardsman paces outside his cell, he consoles himself with the thought that he was not the first of his line to land in jail. The old man had been incarcerated back home, and sprung after just a few months. Brother Willie came awfully close to it, too, but for fleeing when he did. And look at him now! Willie would arrange matters for Robert, by hook or by crook. Or more likely by camera. Willie knew everyone in town. He had fingered them this way and that, proper as you please, all the little touches and tweaks necessary to yield a pretty pose. The ladies as much as the men. Robert won't pine for long at the foot of the current. Willie would have him out in a trice.

As long as Mag had destroyed the letters. As long as no one paid mind to that sanctimonious Robert Murray. Now what exactly had he, Robert Notman, said to him? Impossible to recall the exact words....

Robert's thoughts run in channels of this sort in the morning, as he makes up his straw bed to the clang of the prison bell. Even with the scraping of hundreds of feet marching out to work, the words of the Psalm return to him with their blessed balm. "I will extol Thee, O Lord, for Thou ... hast not suffered mine enemies to rejoice over me."

But at night, when he lies staring at a ceiling he can barely make out with the light seeping in from the peephole in the cell door, at night it's a different refrain.

"'What profit is there in my blood, when I go down to the pit?'"

Had King David ever known a pit like this prison? Oh, it looked grand from outside, a testament to sober justice. To a free man, as he was but a few days ago, it evoked the notion of edification, rather than harsh penalty. Fortunate were those who walked by, ignorant of a cell's weeping walls trapping the dampness of the nearby river, so that beneath a thin blanket barely covering a tall prisoner sleep withheld all promise? He knows that the French convicts whisper among themselves about the dozen Patriotes *whose necks had snapped on the gibbet in the front yard. That was long ago, after the rebellions in the Canadas in 1837, the year of Robert's birth in Paisley. Grisly to reflect upon those hangings thirty years ago, but those events were an eternity removed from his own predicament.*

What haunts Robert is not the dead rebels, but the case of Patterson. For Patterson was a mere seven years past and directly relevant to himself. He remembers the case well. Perhaps... no... – surely rumour of Jesse Patterson's fate had led Dr. Patton to seek succour from a vial of prussic acid. And was there the remotest chance that Patterson's fate would become Robert's?

A mob howled for Patterson's blood in 1861 when, quite possibly, Robert was still teaching Sunday school at the Zion Congregational Church, where in August 1857 he was the 543rd member to be entered in the registry. (Numbers 541 and 542 were, respectively, William and Alice.) In those days he was a model of piety. On Sundays he attended church not once, but twice a day whenever possible. William wrote to

Alice's parents, "We enjoy Dr. Wilkes ministry very much Robert & I were out in the morning & Alice & he are there this Eve." He was also an industrious clerk at Ogilvy & Lewis, the same dry goods firm where William first found employment. Alice commended his diligence in a letter home in April 1857. "Bob is never in till near 12. They are awfully busy now selling £3 & 4000 a day – but Robert likes his place very much, it is a capital place for him to sharpen his wits."

Like William, Robert knew the dry goods business from the ground up, both of them having apprenticed with their father. A Scottish census found him at age fourteen a "warehouse man" in the family business. But he had ambitions to strike out on his own and, like others in his family, was inspired by William's success with photography. At various moments of his life he gave his occupation as artist or photographer. He also carried on a business of his own as an importer or wholesaler of photographic supplies.

A pleasant-looking young man standing five foot ten, with light blue eyes, brown hair, and a fair complexion, he was a member in good standing with his community. On July 30, 1861 Reverend Wilkes married him to Annie Birks, a suitable match for the circumstances of both. Annie – twenty-five to Robert's twenty-four – lived up the street from the Notman studio on Bleury Street. She was the gentle-faced daughter of chemist John Birks and sister of silversmith Henry Birks, the future founder of the iconic Montreal jewelry emporium, Henry Birks and Sons. Members of the Birks family were regular clients of William Notman. As artists and fine craftsmen, Henry Birks and William Notman likely appreciated each other's skills and talents.

Is it reading too much into photographs of Annie Notman taken at the studio the year of her marriage, and then again two years later, to ascribe the stunned eyes, brittle waist, and rigid back in the second picture to unhappiness in her marriage? For by 1862 there were signs of trouble. A note next to Robert's name in the Zion Congregational Church register states that on March 5, 1862 – a mere seven months after the wedding – he was "excommunicated for repeated and deliberate lying." Can we speculate about another woman, or even perhaps other women?

Like a ghostly echo of some long-forgotten secret, an old tale still circulates about Annie and Robert, a century and a half after her death. The apocryphal legend woven around her and her ne'er-do-well groom goes like this. Swaybacked Annie Birks Notman, great with child, waddles to the front door in response to a knock. She gasps in incomprehension, as a woman she has never before seen thrusts a baby at her.

"Here, take it, it's your man's!"

Annie recoils. She begins to holler for help. Her hands instinctively clutch her belly, as beneath the layers of protective fabric that swathe a Victorian lady a jolt of hot pain doubles her over. Her waters break, blood pools beneath her, she miscarries and dies.

An element of this story is unquestionably true. Childless for the first two years of her marriage, Annie delivered a little girl, also named Annie, on March 24, 1864. Six days later Annie, the mother, was dead. Little Annie became a cherished member of the clan, doted upon by Robert's parents and siblings, photographed at all stages of her life, and so well integrated into Notman professional culture that she was one of the family's first female members to work in the studio.

As for the legend, there's no word on what happened to the baby whose introduction to Annie Notman Senior supposedly precipitated the premature arrival of her daughter. Was there ever even such a baby, or is the myth a conflation of some early indiscretions of Robert's with his great scandal of 1868?

Robert next surfaces in the historic record as witness in an arson case in 1865. James A. Watts – listed in the city directory as an importer of American hardware – was accused of setting fire to his shop in Custom House Square. He was clapped in jail until his trial on April 17, which as it happened, was justly overshadowed by an event of shocking historical importance. On April 14 John Wilkes Booth shot the president of the United States in Ford's Theater, and Lincoln died early the next morning in Washington, D.C. Next to the short article about James Watts's trial in the *Gazette*, ran an account of a prayer meeting of 4,000 worshippers commemorating the President's assassination at the Wesleyan Chapel in Great St. James Street.

Watts's shop carried a line of locks, hardware, "plated ware," and placemats. He also had a stock of photographic samples that the prosecution valued at about $200, and was insured for $1,000 with the Scottish Provincial Assurance Company. The fire was discovered around nine-thirty at night on January 30. Eyewitnesses reported that it was extinguished by the application of buckets of snow. Several people testified about the discovery of combustible materials beneath wooden shelving; some swore that it was arson.

At the trial, George Taylor, Watts's office boy, said that when he visited the prisoner in jail, Watts questioned him about what the police had been interested in, and hinted that upon his release they could go into partnership. Taylor also noted that Watts "was in the habit of smoking in the store with his friends."

One of those friends was Robert Notman, who provided Watts with the alibi that led to his acquittal. Though Notman gave his occupation as "artist," he added that he had supplied Watts with the photographic materials in the store to sell on commission. Robert estimated the worth of these supplies at $672, a considerably higher figure than the prosecutor's calculation of $200. Robert said that he and Watts had left the store together at four thirty in the afternoon and that the two of them had gone for a drive along the river to Point St. Charles. The round trip took them an hour and a half, including a stop at a livery stable in Alexander Street to drop off the horse. From there they walked to Eliot Terrace, a short section of St. Catherine Street just east of Bleury where Robert lived with his parents, arriving at six o'clock. Watts visited all evening until quarter to eleven. Robert could vouch for the hour since he remembered spending a few minutes in the parlour alone, then mounting the stairs and hearing the clock strike the hour in his room.

Corroborating this testimony was that of teenaged James Notman, the youngest of the Notman brothers. James confirmed everything Robert had said: Watts had, indeed, been at their house all evening long; James himself had left the house only for five minutes at half past six.

The Notman brothers almost certainly saved Watts's hide, because Judge Mondelet, who presided over the court, was not disposed in his favour. Watts's business was floundering, he owed money to his landlord, and there was plenty of evidence to suggest that the source of the fire was not a cold stove, but a pile of charred sticks jumbled up with a heap of placemats in a poorly ventilated corner of the shop. When the jury returned a verdict of not guilty after a mere half hour of deliberation, "His HONOUR said he could not accept the verdict, and the jury must again return to their room." A stiff-necked juror retorted "that they would remain of the same opinion if locked up to the end of the week."

The judge adjourned proceedings until the next morning, when the jury repeated the original verdict. Mondelet was clearly put out. He stated that "the Court had no right to dictate to the jury," but added balefully that the responsibility of the wrongheaded verdict would have to rest with them.

No one suggested for an instant that Robert Notman was in cahoots with Watts. And yet a man who had been thrown out of his church "for repeated and deliberate lying" was perhaps not the best character witness or alibi provider. It's not beyond the bounds of possibility that the two friends had cooked up a scheme to defraud the insurance company together. Such a thought may have crossed the judge's mind when he sent the jury back to reconsider their decision. As Robert mounted the stairs of his father's house, candle in hand to light his way, and the clock tolled eleven times in his bedroom, was he thinking of splitting the insurance money with Watts and expanding his business? Was he looking forward to having the trappings of a successful business – a summer residence like Clydeside perhaps? And what about marrying again? He and his wife had lived their married life under the same roof as his parents. With an establishment of his own like William's in both business and household, he would be an eligible catch.

But these are mere speculations. For the record, James Watts kept his nose clean after his brush with the law. The following year he remade himself as a travelling agent in the down-market region of St. Henry's Tannery West. But within a couple of years he was back to plying his business as a hardware owner in the same neighbourhood as the store that burned down.

Robert huddles in a corner of his cell in the jail. His teeth are chattering. He gathers the folds of his blanket around his shoulders like a shawl, trying to dispel the images of the nightmare that has scared him awake. The scene in front of the prison. The scaffold, the noose, the drop, the snapping of a neck. Not Patterson's – no, not that – but that of the other blackguard, Alexander Burns, the despicable murderer of a baby boy who was simultaneously his son and grandson. Cheated by the last minute commutation given the abortionist, the mob rampaged, the countrywomen who had streamed to the city for the spectacle of a double execution keening like the seagulls of the port.

On his knees, Robert gazes at the faint light of the watchman's torch through the peephole. He closes his eyes tight, trying to pray. "Joy cometh in the morning, joy cometh in the morning," he whispers. But behind his closed lids he sees handsome Alfred Patton gulping down the blue contents of a vial and quickly arranging his bedclothes around himself with barely time for oblivion to overtake him. He sees his own father laid out on his bier in the parlour of Eliot Terrace.

He staggers to his feet. No good can come from such visions. He wraps the thin blanket around himself like a swaddling cloth and stretches out on his pallet. Somehow, still shivering, he drifts into a condition half sleep, half hallucination. In this limbo state he is once more in the luxury suite on the ground floor of the St. Lawrence Hall with its posh appointments, Mag prone on the feather bed, unconscious. The doctor bends over her, his hand on her wrist, panic on his face as her pulse ebbs.

Robert jolts abruptly awake, gasping for breath. The noose intended for Jesse Patterson's neck is clamped around his own.

[CHAPTER EIGHT]

"Disgusting Details"

THE COURTHOUSE STOOD on Notre Dame Street, its back to the parade grounds of the Champ-de-Mars, its face to the river, its tall rectangular windows framing glimpses of the blue-grey St. Lawrence. Acknowledged as the city's most impressive public building, it was designed in 1856 by John Ostell, Montreal's premier architect of the day, in the mode of high Victorian grandeur. Beneath a gabled roof, six Ionic columns formed a colonnade supporting a central pediment that jutted out of the cut stone structure like a prominent nose in a heavy featured countenance. A mere *house* in the English language, this place of judgement was *le Palais de justice*.

A German tourist saw it not so much as a palace but a Greek temple, "only larger and more massive." The monumental style attested to the gravitas and overarching necessity of the rule of law in a civilized society. The courthouse was the place where those who had (or appeared to have had) fallen foul of the law came to be tried by their peers. Presiding over the proceedings, ruling on the efforts of counsel for the defence to exonerate and for the Crown to convict, teasing apart what was permissible evidence and what not, and ultimately charging the jury as to their course was the awful – "awful" – in its original sense of commanding reverential fear and profound respect – role of the judge. Not for nothing was he referred to as His Honour.

On the morning of Monday April 20, 1868, Lewis Thomas Drummond, the judge who would uphold the honour of the law in the case of the Queen versus Robert Notman, was in a state of high cantankerousness. A brilliant man of many parts and perplexing contradictions, His Honour decried the fact that his courtroom was stuffed to the gills with men, women, and youths, all of them agog to view for themselves the principals of the drama – Miss Galbraith and the imprisoned Mr. Notman – and a notable supporting cast. As the *Gazette* reported the following day, "the list of witnesses ... contains the names of many prominent citizens."

Judge Drummond was well acquainted with the vagaries and frailties of humankind. It was no surprise to him that "the nature of the crime and the social position of the prisoner" made the Notman case a *cause célèbre*. This understanding only heightened the deeply distressing nature of the matter for him. He knew the defendant, sympathized with the Notman family, and held firm views of the crime in question.

For the first hour of the proceedings he dealt with the routine. The prisoner was placed at the bar, the five indictments against him were read, learned counsel were introduced, and jury selection began. The judge was not amused when the lawyers quibbled at length about the composition of the jury, twenty-three men having to be set aside. Finally a dozen were settled upon, sworn, and empanelled. Then Bernard Devlin, chief counsel for Robert Notman, moved for all witnesses in the case to leave the courtroom.

At this point the judge gave vent to an extraordinary little outburst. He called for the strictest order to be kept in the chamber, and waxed sarcastic about the unusual degree of genius required "to put so little accommodation into so large a room." He directed the court constable to clear the place of all women and young people and to forbid their return. He then expressed the hope that "he would not again see scandalous scenes repeated, which he had witnessed when of counsel in the Patterson case in which the most disgusting details occurred."

In the distinguished career of Lewis Thomas Drummond as a jurist, politician, and businessman, the case in which he defended the backroom abortionist Jesse Patterson in 1861 was a mere footnote. But in April 1868, the Patterson case was still fresh in the memory of Montrealers. And quite possibly it still sat heavily on the conscience of the devoutly Catholic judge whose two sons were both Jesuits.

Born in 1813 to a prominent attorney in Coleraine in County Londonderry, Ireland, Drummond crossed the Atlantic with his widowed mother at the age of twelve under unusual circumstances. The boy had a gift for mathematics and when the captain of the ship was taken ill on the voyage, he gave over responsibility for calculating the ship's course to young Lewis.

Drummond also had a ready facility for language. On arrival to Montreal, he learned French quickly and entered the Séminaire de Nicolet, near Joliet, where he studied for six years and was something of an oddity. Despite the ridicule of his fellow students, he insisted on affecting a Parisian accent, a habit that rubs many Quebecers the wrong way to this day.

Drummond elected to follow in his father's footsteps, articling in the offices of Charles Dewey Day, a future chancellor of McGill University and a noted Tory. Dummond's own political tendencies were progressive and, after being called to the bar in 1836, he showed his sympathy for the French-Canadian cause by an able defence of *Patriotes* in the trials that followed the Rebellion of 1837. A superb and flashy orator, he entered politics as a LaFontaine Reformer in the 1840s, but he never stuck close to any particular party line. At the same time as he hobnobbed with the French seigneurial class (his wife was a francophone landed heiress), he championed the Irish workers who built the Lachine Canal. Though he spent sixteen years in the legislative assembly of United Canada and served as both Solicitor General and Attorney General, he persisted in marching to his own drumbeat. Courting certain defeat at the polls, for instance, at a time of great tension with the United States in the early 1860s, he took a prophetic stance in declaring that "the best armament for Canada was no armament at all." He was named to the bench in 1864, which is how he came to play a decisive role in the life of Robert Notman.

The case of Jesse Patterson – popularly known as "the Clarenceville Murder Trial" – was a burlesque overture to the Notman affair. The events which prompted it took place among poor and uneducated people in a village in southwestern Quebec. The fact that Clarenceville was close to the border with Vermont gave rise to widespread fears that an American abortion epidemic was heading north. This was a theme that would dominate the trial of Robert Notman as well.

Unlike Dr. Alfred Patton, Jesse Patterson had a shoddy reputation as a physician and was known for performing abortions. But Patterson was charged with murder, not abortion. Olive Savariat, the unfortunate sixteen-year-old whom he took in unscrupulous hand first when she was about four months pregnant and then again at an appalling seven months, died some six weeks after his ministrations.

Aside from its sensational nature, the Clarenceville murder trial was noteworthy for pitting two fine legal minds against each other. Lewis Thomas Drummond was regarded as the best criminal lawyer at the time in the province. The prosecutor, Francis (later Sir Francis) Johnson, was his match in every way. Like Drummond an immigrant, Johnson had more privileged credentials. Born into a gentry family in Bedfordshire, England, he attended Harrow, the famous public school, and then studied in France and Belgium. Like Drummond, he also trained in the office of Charles Dewey Day and would later become a judge.

The advancement of both lawyers was paved by their splendid command of French. More than thirty years after the Patterson trial, a historian recalled how both "held the crowded Court House entranced with the charm of their French speeches."

Because Jesse Patterson spoke English, an English jury was sworn, but many key witnesses testified in French, which then had to be translated for the benefit of the prisoner and the jury. At one point Johnson bemoaned the fact "that the evidence, having to be translated, did not reach the jury with the force that it reached the learned counsel's ears." For this reason, at times the English papers quoted the most startling testimony in its French original. Citing Olive Savariat's bitter words on her deathbed about the man who had seduced her, and then paid Patterson to abort her against her will, Olive's mother testified, "*Comme il est chetif* [sic] *James Collins, il est la cause de ma mort. Il aimerait mieux donner trente piastres pour faire mourir mon enfant, plutot* [sic] *que de me le donner pour le faire vivre.*" ("James Collins caused my death because he is such a miser. He'd rather give thirty dollars to have my child die, than give money to me so I can bring him up.")

Drummond based his defence of Patterson on the argument that much of the evidence was hearsay and that there was an absence of intent to kill on his client's part. He argued that Olive died as a consequence of consumption, peritonitis, and/or inflammation of the uterus resulting from a natural delivery. But Patterson's reputation, popular sympathy for the key witness – Olive's grief-stricken mother – and the gory nature of the evidence made the job of defence uphill work.

Seven years after Patterson was condemned to death and Robert Notman stood in the prisoner's box, the "scandalous scenes" and "disgusting details" in the earlier case remained vivid in Drummond's mind.

What might the judge have deemed to be scandalous and disgusting?

Item: after a complaint by a local magistrate that Olive came to her death through ill treatment, her body was exhumed three-and-a half weeks subsequent to her death on Shrove Tuesday, February 12, 1861. At the trial, the results of the post-mortem were made public: "there had been a foetus but there was no evidence of its expulsion in the natural way, it appeared as if some instrument, not sharp, had been resorted to." The doctor conducting the autopsy declared that Olive died as a result of "inflammation of the womb, and its appendages and such inflammation had been caused by unnatural means."

Item: during her first month of pregnancy, "James Collins gave her medicine strong enough to burn the inside of a horse which he had procured from Patterson."

Item: Olive was visibly pregnant in October, 1860, having worked as a servant in the household of James Collins's parents for several months. The Collinses lived two or three miles out of Clarenceville. Olive used to go home to her mother's every couple of weeks.

Item: In view of the fact that the drugs administered weren't effective, James Collins and Patterson repeatedly took her into the Collins barn "and performed operations on her with an instrument which gave her great pain."

Item: Olive told her mother that "God knows I was not willing that Collins should do that, but he promised to marry me."

Item: Collins called in on Patterson "two or three times a week to put an end to the child."

Item: In mid-December, Olive was hired to work as a servant in the Patterson household.

Item: On or around December 13, when Olive was six and a half months gone, Patterson administered drugs to her "designed to procure an abortion."

Item: A week or so later her mother visited her and found her "sick on a truckle bed," having "lost her colour and most of her blood." Mme Savariat understood right away that "she was then no longer with child." Patterson later claimed that Olive had gone into premature labour at four months and that he delivered her of a dead foetus. "Would it not be my duty to take that child from her and save her character?"

Item: Olive's thirteen-year-old brother, Jean-Baptiste, was already working in the Patterson household when Olive came to stay there. On the night she was delivered, he heard her crying. Jean-Baptiste drove Olive home in a sleigh the following day.

Item: Mme Savariat testified that after "eight days or so" at home, Olive began to spit blood. She never got out of bed again "and for two or three weeks before her death continually vomited and spat up blood."

Item: a few days before Olive's death, she had a consultation with another doctor at Patterson's behest. Dr. Brigham said nothing could be done for her by then. A priest administered the sacraments. Olive made her confession and received extreme unction.

Item: Jean Baptiste heard Olive say to her mother after the priest's departure, "It would not have been so bad had the child been buried in the ordinary way instead of having been burned."

On the first day of the Notman trial, Judge Lewis Thomas Drummond may well have cast his thoughts back to the man who had presided over the Patterson case, the colourful and mercurial Thomas Cushing Aylwin. Aylwin was royally put out when witnesses failed to show up because of the erection of a hustings near the courthouse. He threatened that any sheriff who might subsequently allow electioneering close to a trial over which he sat would be fined up to a thousand dollars, adding that "between the noise and turmoil of an election, and the sitting of a Court wherein life and death was pending, there was nothing in common."

"Short, nearsighted, and ... never quite sober, Aylwin commanded not by his physical presence as much as by his charming, genial bluffness and, above all, by his prodigious bilingual gift for words," writes the author of the entry on Aylwin in the *Dictionary of Canadian Biography*. But when it came to Patterson, Aylwin was in no charming or genial frame of mind. In his charge to the jury he pointed to the law respecting murder, and having taken a broad interpretation of that law, he then went on to discuss the prevalence of abortion "especially in the locality where … [Patterson] had resided, … which he characterized as second to the state of Sodom and Gomorrha." The situation threatened to "overturn the very foundations on which civilized society rested."

Newspapers commenting on Aylwin's charge noted that in every respect it discounted the defence's case, and concluded with the instruction to the jury that "they incline against the prisoner.… They had a solemn public duty to perform, and one from which they must not shrink however painful it might be to their feelings."

The jury deliberated for only an hour and a half before bringing in the guilty verdict, and the judge then pronounced the death sentence. He went on to warn in the strongest terms about the "deplorable state to which society would be reduced if such crimes as the prisoner had committed were to become frequent, dwelling with strong effect on the wickedness of the man who, for thirty dollars, had destroyed the lives of two human beings, and sent to the grave, burdened with ignominy, and pointed at with scorn, a young and beautiful girl, destined, perhaps, but for his baneful arts, to lead a long and happy life."

Victorian judges and juries had a certain amount of sympathy for the plight of seduced and abandoned girls, especially ones like Olive Savariat, who wanted to bring up her child but did not have the financial wherewithal. Because society had a convenient scapegoat in Patterson, the law seems to have ignored the instigator of the crime: James Collins, Olive's seducer. Just the opposite would happen in the Notman case.

Patterson was sentenced to hang on September 6, 1861, on the gallows in front of the same Montreal jail where Robert Notman would be incarcerated in 1868. There were two miscreants scheduled for execution on the same day and by early morning a mob had gathered for the spectacle. According to the *Gazette,* "the streets in the neighbourhood of the gaol were densely crowded, and the house tops overlooking the scaffold and gaol yard fairly covered with spectators, a great many of whom – nearly one half – were women."

The Burns and Patterson trials had dominated the newspapers over the course of the summer. Convicted for the crime of murdering his newborn son – a child borne him by his daughter – Alexander Burns had no plea for clemency. But Patterson's case was murkier and elicited controversy. A petition was launched asking for a commutation of his sentence from death to life imprisonment. Letters to the editor questioned whether Olive had died of the direct or even indirect effects of the abortion she had undergone. "We rejoice," said one, "that the law has caught one who we understand has been a professed abortionist for years, in that part of the country where he resided. That Patterson is essentially a bad man we have no doubt; that he cannot tell the truth even to save his life, we have we fear some evidence of. But ... we cannot look upon him as a murderer."

Such subtleties did not preoccupy the throng that awaited its grisly thrills. The first act of the expected double bill did not disappoint. Burns came out of the jail and was escorted to the scaffold and placed on the drop. At the prompting of the priests and nuns present, he recited his final prayers. But a glitch in the mechanics of the execution led to a long drawn-out suffocation instead of a neat snap of the neck.

This bonus of agony for those who relished the sight of suffering did not dampen the mob's enthusiasm for the expected encore. They were counting on Patterson to follow in Burns's footsteps. Many country women from the Clarenceville area had come to see him die. A poem castigating him for having "deprived of baptism a poor innocent being," was making the rounds. But, unknown to the crowd, the Governor General had commuted Patterson's sentence to life imprisonment the evening before. And when Patterson failed to materialize, the crowd rampaged. "Women and children were knocked down and run over," the *Gazette* reported. "The carriages in the street ran against each other, and five or six were seriously injured; and some people were trampled upon so heavily that their limbs were dislocated, and we understand that several were broken ... A great many articles of dress were lost in the confusion, but afterwards claimed at the police station, mostly by women from the country."

Petty criminals took advantage of the general mayhem. "Executions," said the *Herald*, "are notorious as being favoured with the presence of pickpockets, and yesterday's did not prove an exception. Several parties called at the police station in the course of the afternoon and left descriptions of watches, etc., of which they had been robbed in the crowd."

Meanwhile, the *Gazette* speculated that Patterson must have "suffered the tortures of the damned when he heard their cries and probably the boom of the falling trap on which his fellow convict suffered." Though his neck was saved, he was destined to spend the rest of his days at the Provincial Penitentiary in Kingston. What fate lay in store seven years later for Robert Notman?

CHAPTER NINE

"Sodom and Gomorrha"

THE WORDS "SODOM AND GOMORRHA" became a rallying cry after Judge Aylwin made the association between abortion in the border village of Clarenceville and the Biblical twin cities of sexual depravity. "Of the various crimes, in the long category of them, we regard abortion as the most pernicious in its effects upon society," trumpeted the *British American Journal* in July 1861. "Its tendency is demoralising in the highest degree; and when it is perpetrated on an extensive scale, as we much fear it is in certain places or districts in the United States, such places ... are in a condition of immorality rivalling that of a 'Sodom and Gomorrha'. We have been informed that the practice is common even among the better classes in the States, and that it is a rare thing now to find a family with more than two children. We regret exceedingly that this vile practice has crept into Canada, and has found here imitators."

Holding the fate of Robert Notman in his hands seven years later, Judge Lewis Thomas Drummond thundered from the bench, "It is the duty of every parent to crush out this germ of destruction, this moral epidemic which is coming up in our midst, and has ... contaminated the Townships."

Margaret Galbraith came from South Stukely in the Eastern Townships, the exact region of vice the judge was singling out. South Stukeley lay some sixty miles northeast of Clarenceville. From the vantage point of the city of Montreal, the two communities were in the same neighbourhood.

"It is time that something should be done by the public and the Courts to arrest this most terrible of crimes," railed Judge Drummond, calling it the felony of felonies, the one that par excellence struck a "deadly ... blow at the root and foundation of all society."

Clearly abortion was a hot-button issue for the courts, for the newspapers, and for most members of the medical profession. Yet evidence also exists that not all of society shared the view voiced by an American doctor some twenty years after the Notman case: "Better, far better, to bear a child every year for twenty years than to resort to such a wicked and injurious step; better to die; if needs be, in the pangs of child-birth, than to live with such a weight of sin on the conscience."

Abortion as a tool of birth control has a long history. The Hippocratic Oath was interpreted by physicians as a proscription against the practice, but Hippocrates himself wrote of methods to induce miscarriage. Through the ages, when methods such as strenuous physical activity and herbal remedies – the stock-in-trade of midwives and other experienced wise women – failed, infanticide was another option.

Nonetheless, until the early nineteenth century, abortion – along with other methods of contraception – was treated as a private concern in Britain and its colonies. In *The Nature of Their Bodies: Women and Their Doctors in Victorian Canada*, historian Wendy Mitchinson catalogues abstinence, sterilization, pessaries, herbal concoctions, vaginal sponges, diaphragms, condoms, coitus interruptus, coitus obstructus, coitus reservatus, douching, prolonged breastfeeding, and a primitive version of the rhythm method among methods used at that time.

In 1803 England passed its first piece of legislation outlawing abortion. Historians are divided over whether before that time common law provided for protection of the foetus, but the general consensus seems to be that common law allowed for abortion at least before "quickening" – that first time a baby's movement in the uterus is detected by its mother. Canadian legal historian Constance Backhouse writes that the British act of 1803 – which became the model for subsequent statutes in British North America –"specifically prohibited abortions upon women *who had already quickened*, something about which the common law had been unclear. However the major significance of the act was its criminalization of abortions on women who had not yet quickened. The latter had never previously been viewed as criminal. The penalties reflected this situation; those who procured abortions after quickening were subject to death as felons, while those who procured them before quickening faced a lesser sentence…." These included fines, imprisonment, whipping or transportation from the mother country for up to fourteen years.

Paradoxically juries tended to be much more lenient towards the perpetrators of infanticide than towards those performing abortions. Backhouse explains, "With infanticide trials, skillful counsel could rouse a great deal of sympathy for the distressed woman in the prisoner's dock. Abortion trials typically focused on the abortionist, not the immediate desperation of an unwillingly pregnant woman."

The earliest Canadian colonies to pattern legislation on the British Act were New Brunswick in 1810 and Prince Edward Island in 1836. It's not clear why such legislation was passed because no evidence exists to suggest that people at large were preoccupied with the subject. Nor was there any attempt to enforce the law; no cases of abortion trials in Canada have surfaced in the early part of the century. Historian Angus McLaren insists that "women clung to the traditional view that life was not present until the foetus 'quickened'. They did not perceive themselves as pregnant, but as 'irregular'. They took pills not to abort, but to 'bring on their period.'"

And there were plenty of pills to choose from. A profusion of patent medicines advertised in Montreal's English newspapers in the 1860s claimed to cure all female plaints and problems. Holloway's Pills, for instance, reassured "Mothers and Daughters" that "Universally adopted as the one grand remedy for female complaints, they never fail, never weaken the system and always bring about what is required." "Always bring about what is required" can be interpreted as code for producing a miscarriage. Dr. Radway's Pills also supposedly cured "all complaints of women," including "suppression of the menses." Either these medicines contained compounds of iron and mercury intended to act as emetics and purgatives bringing on severe vomiting, fever, and diarrhea, or they were made of ergot, which had long been in use to induce labour. That they were dangerous for the person ingesting them goes without saying. "Nothing that is swallowed can cause abortion without also causing death or severe disability to the mother," writes social historian Peter Gossage.

Among the many changes revolutionizing society during the nineteenth century was the displacement of female midwives by male doctors from the arena of the birth canal. Physicians won this turf war by the defamation of so-called ignorant women and by their own claims of superior expertise. (An excellent fictional depiction of this professional competition is found in Ami McKay's novel *The Birth House*.) Vying for the birth business with midwives, doctors had a vested interest in a high birth rate, and extolled women's role as the bearers of children. Backhouse writes that – as the century wore on – the idea of a "professionalization" of domesticity emerged. A "pervasive cult of motherhood" was preached from the pulpit by churchmen of various stripes. "No love, not even the tenderest" could surpass a mother's, claimed a Halifax minister in 1856. "Forgetful of herself, her sole care is centred on this little object...." Many women eagerly embraced this sanctified ethos as evidence of their own moral superiority. "Our little ones come to us and by their very helplessness appeal to all that is pure and holy, all that is tender and loving in our natures..." maintained a Mrs. Gordon Grant at a Woman's Christian Temperance convention in 1888.

The cult of childbearing, however, clashed with the strict social code that punished and ostracized those who fell foul of it. This was particularly true for a middle-class city girl. A Margaret Galbraith, enrolled at the McGill Normal School, faced a crushing fall from grace. By breaking the rules, her aspirations to be a teacher would be stillborn. If abandoned by her lover, she would likely be cut off from family and friends. How then to support herself and her child? Failing the charity of others, she was headed for a career in a brothel.

The idealization of motherhood also hit a wall when it came to the stark realities of giving birth. In general, nineteenth-century birthing was a crude, excruciating, and often deadly event. Doctors and midwives spread childbirth fever to their unsuspecting patients with their septic hands. Awkward interventions with forceps and instruments frequently led to trauma and/or death. While most young married women must have anticipated having children as the natural fulfilment of their role in life, the prospect of labour and delivery would have also elicited an equally natural dread of pain and possible death. It seems far-fetched to assume that they looked forward with delight to an unending succession of pregnancies.

A startling letter from Queen Victoria – that emblem of moral rectitude, who brought nine children into the world – sheds some clarity on what childbirth meant even to the most privileged of females. Writing in January 1841, the twenty-one-year-old monarch thanked her uncle, the King of Belgium, for his good wishes upon the birth of her first child. She then reproached him for wishing to see her the "Mamma d'une nombreuse famille," for, she added, "I think you will see with me the great inconvenience of a *large* family would be to us all, and particularly to the country, independent of the hardship and inconvenience to myself." Most telling is Victoria's plaintive cry: "[M]en never think; at least seldom think, what a hard task it is for us women to go through this *very often.*"

It is of course a huge leap from the Queen's bedchamber to the ministrations of abortionists. But abortionists were very busy south of the Canadian border around the time that the Queen of England was bringing forth her family. In New York City a notorious Madame Restell advertised blatantly in the press and carried on such a successful practice that the tabloid *National Police Gazette* mounted a publicity campaign against her. When she was brought to trial in 1847 and sentenced to a year's imprisonment, she served it under flagrantly easy conditions because of her cosy relationship with law enforcement officers. Many – though by no means all – of her clients were prostitutes. In *Abortion Rites: A Social History of Abortion in America,* Marvin Olasky calculates that on the eve of the Civil War there were in the United States at least one hundred thousand prostitution-related abortions *per year.*

In the 1860s several popular American books decried abortion in language strikingly similar to that of judges Aylwin and Drummond. In 1862, James C. Jackson's *The Sexual Organism, and Its Healthful Management* called abortion "among the greatest of crimes." Published in 1867, *The Great Crime of the Nineteenth Century* by Edwin M. Hale stated that abortion was both a crime against physiology and a crime against morality that should be labelled no less than murder.

In the early 1870s, the *New York Times* and *New York Tribune* both took up cudgels against abortion with front-page headlines such as THE EVIL OF THE AGE and THE ROOT OF THE EVIL. When – at the age of sixty-five, Madame Restell, a New York abortionist who flaunted her money, was once again arrested, the *Times* claimed that her clients belonged "to the wealthiest families."

In light of this context, the words of the Montreal editorialist who observed in 1861 "that the practice is common even among the better classes in the States, and that it is a rare thing now to find a family with more than two children" may be seen more clearly. Abortion among the lower classes showed moral turpitude, but it was far more troubling if practiced among "the better classes." Constance Backhouse writes that in Canada "a sharp fall in the middle class English birthrate had already begun to generate anxiety, especially when inflamed by fear about the fertility of the Irish, the Quebec French, and the influx of non-British immigrants." As the century wore on, "Along with rhetoric about 'foeticide' and 'traffickers in human life,'" commentators and physicians seemed particularly worried about the declining birthrate among the so-called "respectable classes." They decried the prevalence of abortion in affluent circles, claiming that the main reason for the phenomenon was that large families were unfashionable.

Among popular ideas circulating in the United States at mid-century was spiritism, whose adherents not only believed in the possibility of making contact with the dead, but embraced theories of free love and natural passion. Writing in 1867, the Ohio physician Dr. E. M. Buckingham found a direct connection between abortion and "fashionable and intellectual communities." One idea being bruited about was that pregnancies resulting from free unions of like-minded couples or "affinity-mates" should be aborted. Thomas Nichols, an erstwhile spiritist, whose wife, Mary Gove Nichols, had been a gynecologist and abortion counseor in her free love days, argued in the book *Esoteric Anthropology* that there was "no reason why anyone should be compelled to bear children who wishes to avoid it." Published in 1853, the title became a best-seller, with 250,000 copies sold over the course of twenty years.

Spiritism was a popular and powerful movement with intellectually influential supporters. Harriet Beecher Stowe, for instance, was married to a medium and was a sympathizer. Henry Wadsworth Longfellow, Henry Ward Beecher, and Horace Greeley all attended séances in the 1850s and 1860s. Olasky estimates that some two million Americans out of the total population of thirty million adopted spiritist beliefs and engaged in public meetings that passed radical resolutions. Among those taken by the "Free Convention" in Rutland, Vermont in 1858 was "That the most sacred and important right of woman, is her right to decide for herself how often and under what circumstances she shall assume the responsibilities and be subject to the cares and sufferings of Maternity...."

One of the speakers at this Vermont convention was the abolitionist and pacifist Henry Wright, author of *The Unwelcome Child or The Crime of an Undesigned Maternity*. The book was a sustained plea for abortion where a child was unwanted. Wright also proposed that only planned children should come into the world, declaring that a child's "first claim is to a *designed* existence, if it is to exist at all."

Though it is difficult to determine the impact of such progressive ideas on the general public, for about twenty years the spiritists were a strong minority current of opinion among educated and fashionable Americans. Olasky attributes 45,000 abortions to members of the group over this period. Even a century and a half later and even for those holding liberal views on women's reproductive freedom, the reasons for many of these abortions are questionable. According to one physician writing in Maine, young wives were requesting abortions so that they would not miss out on "society and literary associations." And then there was Emily Dickinson's sister-in-law, Susan Dickinson, who must surely have been an extreme example. She thought it "disgusting to have children" and had at least four abortions with a "Dr. Breck of Springfield." That such cases were documented (in this case by Susan's husband, Emily's brother, Austin) underlines a troubling trend.

If even faint traces of these notions drifted across the Vermont and New York borders to Canada, the hysterical reaction to the Patterson and Notman cases becomes more understandable. And one of the reasons the Notman trial attracted the notoriety that it did was because a member of the "better classes," a gentleman who had the wherewithal to hire a well-regarded doctor and to put up his lover in a suite in the city's best hotel, now stood shackled for all to gape at in the prisoner's box at the *Palais de justice*.

CHAPTER TEN

Miss Galbraith

HE SAW THE GIRL *on the platform before she became aware of him. She stood out not merely as a solitary figure at the Bonaventure Station, she stood out because she was beautiful. Of medium height, with the kind of womanly figure that especially appealed to him after the boniness of his late wife, she wore her brown hair in two fat braids down her back, a touch of the Old Country. She had a heart-shaped face, high cheekbones and a determined set to her chin. As he drew closer, he noticed that there was a smudge of soot on that determined chin. She must not have had recourse to a mirror after the long train ride from Waterloo. Shoulders squared, she appeared to be guarding a large black and battered travelling trunk. Despite its dents and scratches, someone had made the effort to polish the metal clasps until they shone.*

"Miss Galbraith?"

Though she had clearly been waiting for someone to fetch her, she startled from head to toe.

"Sorry to be so late.... I'm Robert Notman. I've come from Mrs. Notman to take you to your lodgings.... Let me help you with your trunk."

That battered trunk with its shiny hinges would be the undoing of Robert Notman a few months later – but only the most clairvoyant of mediums or patient of sleuths reading events backwards, not forwards as they are lived – could have intuited that.

I have imagined this meeting this way because I know that Margaret Galbraith came to Montreal in the late summer of 1867 and worked as a servant in the home of the senior Notmans. From the faint traces that Robert has left behind, I can deduce that he had a chronic problem with lateness. But I have no clear indication of how they actually first met, nor how Margaret gained entrée to the Notman household. Perhaps it was through the agency of the St. Andrew's Society or one of the Presbyterian churches. Like much of the story, it is cloaked in mystery.

When researchers at the McCord Museum told me that Margaret came from the Eastern Townships hamlet of South Stukely, I leapt to the conclusion that she was old-stock Loyalist, descended from the disaffected New England settlers who formed the bulk of the inhabitants of Quebec's Shefford County. I was only disabused of this notion when I tracked her down in the records of the McGill University Normal School, led there by a stray clue in the Montreal *Gazette*, a throwaway line indicating that the woman at the heart of the abortion scandal was believed to be studying there.

Founded by a bequest from the Scots-born fur trader James McGill some forty-six years before Margaret and Robert met, McGill preens itself on being one of the oldest and best of Canadian universities. But alongside its reputation for excellence, McGill is also well known for its love of red tape. At first the gatekeepers of the university's archives seemed determined to deny access. The preliminaries for admission to the reading room included a string of petitioning e-mails, a visit to establish credentials, signed requests for select volumes located off-site from the McLennan Library where the archives are housed, special searches for "lost" ledgers which subsequently were miraculously "found."

But it was all worth it when finally – my fingers chastely cloaked in white cotton gloves and clumsily wielding a prescribed standard issue pencil – I cracked open the fragile yellowing vellum pages of the register in which the vital statistics of the "pupil-teachers" who had had the temerity to apply to the school a century and a half ago were inscribed by hand.

Listed thirty-first in a class of forty-nine predominantly female students entering the Normal School in the fall of 1867, was "Margt" Galbraith, at age twenty-four one of the oldest in the group. She gave her permanent residence as the Eastern Townships town of Waterloo, her religion as Canadian Presbyterian, and her place of birth as Scotland.

No old-stock Loyalist as I had presumed, Margaret Galbraith, like William and Robert Notman, was a new immigrant. Within a few hours, courtesy of the Internet, I had tracked her down to the parish of Kilmaronock in Dumbartonshire. (Kilmaronock, not the far more famous Kilmarnock in Ayrshire, home of Robbie Burns's first publisher and of Johnnie Walker whiskey.) She was born on April 4, 1843 to Archibald and Margaret Galbraith, the oldest of ten children, the first seven, like herself, all in Dumbartonshire.

Kilmaronock parish extended over an area of nearly 15,000 acres, encompassing parts of fabled Loch Lomond. *Black's Picturesque Tourist of Scotland*, a guidebook dated 1863, waxed hyperbolic about "the Lake full of islands," the surrounding "dusky and retreating mountains," and the "fair and fertile land" along its shores.

The Galbraith name was common in the region. Among the thirty islands that dot this pride of Scottish lakes is Inch Galbraith. Its chieftains were a warlike lot in the fifteenth and sixteenth centuries, much given to "haitrent and malice." An early-twentieth-century account of their exploits observes that "the Galbraiths... seem to have had a fatal tendency to espouse a losing cause, and to this may be attributed their downfall." *A fatal tendency to espouse a losing cause.* Maybe it ran in the blood.

Today Loch Lomond is one of Scotland's prime tourist destinations, the heart of its first national park. But it was already a hub for vacationers in the early nineteenth century, after Sir Walter Scott's epic best-selling poem *Lady of the Lake* stamped it into public consciousness.

Kilmaronock derived its name from the Gaelic for "Church of my little Ronan," Ronan being an eighth-century saint. Scott made the heroine of the *Lady of the Lake*, a "votaress of Morannan's cell" – a nod of his romantic imagination to the ancient history of the parish and to the fine views of the loch from Ross Priory, the mansion where he stayed. Less than twenty miles south of Glasgow, the seat of the Notmans, it was yet a world apart from the noisy, industrialized, heavily populated capital with its teeming shipyards and factories. "Little Ronan's" church was long gone by the nineteenth century, replaced by two warring Presbyterian establishments vying for the souls of local worshippers, one built in 1813 and the other in 1852. Near one of the churches stood the ruins of Kilmaronock Castle and a few noble mansions, including that of the Duke of Montrose, who owned majestic Ben Lomond. The region had hilly pastures grazed by black-faced sheep and cattle, acres of forest, shallow moors, and plenty of rich, fertile, and arable soil.

A woman who farmed in the area for two decades after World War II wrote in 1971, "Agriculture is its livelihood, and the even tenor of its rural round of seed time and harvest, mating and reproducing, hasn't changed much for the past 2000 years." Nor probably has the placid appearance of the countryside I explored while trying to walk in Margaret Galbraith's footsteps a century and a half after she had left Scotland. On a moody day in August 2012, beneath a low grey sky, the green fields were dotted with spiky purple thistles and brambles of pink wild roses. Blackberry canes hung over stone fences mortared with moss, and leggy wild phlox nodded in the breeze. Even when a gentle rain began to fall, it was peaceful and idyllic.

Archibald Galbraith was a farmer, with a clear attachment to his roots. We have to parse his nature from the scantest of clues. The stark epitaph on his grave in the South Stukely cemetery reads "Native of Dumbartonshire." If we take his own reckoning of his age at face value – his gravestone reads 1795, but census information dates his birth as either 1800 or 1802 – he was sixty-nine at the time of the move. It could not have been easy for him to leave the rolling hills and neat hedgerows of his bucolic countryside, with its gentle climate of easterly winds and light showers, rare heavy rains or frosts, and snow that lasted only on mountaintops. Meaning it as a compliment, Judge Drummond would call him a Puritan at the end of the trial. Yet when Archibald's daughter's shame became the news of the day, the seventy-three-year-old patriarch made the arduous trip from his Townships home to sit by her side in hospital. It may be that he also attended the trial. What little we know of him suggests loyalty, compassion, and deep religious feeling.

Archibald's wife, Margaret Aitken, was a quarter-century his junior. When their first child, our Margaret, was born in 1843, her father was already forty-eight. Two more girls and four sons made up the family's Scottish brood; three additional children became native Canadians. Little William, born in Canada East in 1864, died a year later.

Tucked away in an obscure file among the Notman papers at the McCord Museum is an affidavit by the minister of Archibald and Margaret's Scottish church. In an even, sloping hand it states that "Archibald Galbraith, & his wife, leave the United Presbyterian Congregation of Kilmaronock, at this date in full communion with the United Presbyterian Church." Dated June 8, 1864, the testimonial was meant to pave the way for the Galbraith family to join a similar congregation in the remote parts where they were headed.

But why did they leave? To his dying day Archibald hearkened back to his love of his native county. "Native of Dumbartonshire" was how he chose to be remembered. He was a farmer; the place of his birth was famous for its abundant and rich soil; he was approaching the biblical threescore and ten. And yet at an age when he might be expected to sit back by the hearth and suck on his pipe, he uprooted himself and his family and became a pioneer.

Economic dislocation may have but did not necessarily prompt the departure. Unlike the unfortunate crofters of the Highlands, who were evicted by the tens of thousands from their ancestral plots in the eighteenth and nineteenth centuries to create profitable sheep farms for their landowners, tenant farmers in the Lowlands were relatively prosperous. Historian T. M. Devine describes rural Lowlanders as being much given to moving around within their own region. (The example of William Notman, the "Cowfeeder" comes to mind.) "The rural Scots were very mobile abroad, in large part because they were also very mobile at home…. People in country farms and villages searching for opportunities elsewhere seem to have been able to weigh the attractions of the Scottish towns against those of overseas destinations and come to the decision on the basis of these comparisons…."

As a result of a depression in the 1820s following the Napoleonic wars, many Scots were drawn to the Eastern Townships of Lower Canada by generous land grants. A decade later the enterprising businessman and future Father of Confederation Alexander Tilloch Galt was influential in the colonization activities of the British American Land Company in the area around Sherbrooke, the first major centre of the Townships. The idea was to boost the English-speaking population of Lower Canada in the ever precarious linguistic balancing act that dogged the province. By the mid-1840s Galt was heavily into promoting railways and making sure that the fledgling St. Lawrence and Atlantic Railroad – a key component of the future Grand Trunk – would cross the Townships on its way to Portland, Maine.

In 1860 Galt, by then Finance Minister of the Province of United Canada, published a promotional tract touting the political and economic advantages of the colony to the British public. "Leading roads are opened by the Government into remoter parts of the Province, and free grants of land are made upon them – the price of ordinary land in the Eastern Townships is fixed at 70 cents, or about 3s. Sterling, per acre, for cash, or 4s. sterling (1 dollar), if on credit.… By these arrangements, it is within the power of almost everyone to become the proprietor of a farm, with a free title for ever, and subject to no other charges than the settlers themselves, under the municipal system choose to impose…."

Did Archibald Galbraith read this essay or hear about it from cronies? Had he been mulling the question of emigration for years? Some 170,000 Scots crossed the Atlantic between 1815 and 1870. From mid-century on, the majority of them preferred to settle in Canada rather than the Maritime colonies. Surely Archibald knew that Scottish Lowlanders were preferred immigrants, and not only by dint of their numbers. Their way had been paved by earlier waves of Scottish fur traders and merchants and by Scots-born or -educated physicians and ministers. By Archibald's time, Scots shepherds, ploughmen, and tenant farmers were valued in a country with abundant land but a dearth of skilled labour.

In Scotland even wealthy tenants had trouble acquiring land outright from their landowners, but in Canada a farmer could own land and be confident of being able to bequeath it to the next generation. This may have been at the root of the "Native of Dumbartonshire's" decision to transplant his family.

Like other communities in Lower Canada near the American border, South Stukely was initially colonized by settlers from Massachusetts and Vermont who had remained loyal to the British Crown after the American Revolution. The brunt of the pioneer experience of opening up the region – clearing land, building roads and mills, establishing a framework for community life – was borne by these early colonists. The 1830s saw a wave of French-Canadian settlement, and the hamlet assumed the character of a small village. By the 1850s a railway linked Waterloo – the closest town to Stukely – to Montreal, and new subdivisions were created. A tame, soft landscape not dissimilar to the one back home greeted the Galbraiths. The green rolling countryside was studded with ponds, rivulets, and small lakes in the lee of the western foothills of the Appalachians. There was a shimmering great lake nearby – Memphremagog – and Orford, a looming mountain. There was rich farmland and abundant forests. The church and the schoolhouse were built of stone, like back home. A handsome brick hotel, a post office, three sawmills, and a general store were some of the amenities to be found in the village that a stagecoach connected to neighbouring townships. According to the census of 1861, greater Stukely – there was a North Stukely as well – had a population of 2,320. Scattered over an acreage of ten square miles, the actual dwellings were few and far between.

So a new life, but one that resonated with echoes of the old. Loins to gird, sleeves to roll up: as one contemporary observer noted, "though the labor of clearing a farm is considerable, when once the work is effected, the land is very productive."

The reputation for hard work and industriousness for which Scottish immigrants were prized had its origins in the history of the Reformation in Scotland in the sixteenth century. Imported from Switzerland by the son of a Scottish farmer, it was a grassroots movement. The Lowlands embraced John Knox's fervent and authoritarian brand of Protestantism with its emphasis on sin, blasphemy, and ineluctable predestination. Yet the harshness of Presbyterianism was mitigated by the promise of direct access to God.

"Knox and his supporters were uncompromising Calvinists who believed that man's whole life is to be lived to the glory of God," writes the twentieth-century Canadian academic and stalwart Presbyterian minister W. Stanford Reid in *The Scottish Tradition in Canada*. "This, however, could be done only by the way in which the Christian knew God's will for him through the guidance of the Holy Spirit speaking in Holy Writ."

Because of this belief that the Bible was an open book for anyone able to read, Scottish culture came to be grounded in near universal literacy. By the end of the eighteenth century education had a much broader base in Scotland than in any other European country. And there was a direct connection between an ethos of religiously inspired learning and economic development. According to Reid, tough-mindedness, dutifulness and a desire for self-improvement were all part of the Calvinist and Puritan ethic. "[A Scot] whatever his background, social and economic origins, felt that he had the right and duty to make the best of himself and to rise in the world. One can think of farming families which have produced ministers, doctors, lawyers, nurses and school teachers."

Reid's father grew up on a farm in the Eastern Townships in the latter part of the nineteenth century and would eventually become a minister. In the Reid home everyone gathered on Sundays to recite the Westminster Shorter Catechism, a series of 107 questions and answers inculcating Calvinist doctrines. In the "Puritan" Galbraith household, Margaret and her siblings were probably similarly raised.

Scottish Protestants stressed the importance of developing one's God-given attributes regardless of social distinctions and class structure. One sure way was by acquiring technical training or higher education. Though British North America did not have the array of choices that Scotland offered, there were still several avenues for those who had exhausted the possibilities of the one-room schoolhouse. One big factor in selecting a school of higher learning was the presence of other Scots in the student body and among the professors. At Quebec's Morrin College, Montreal's McGill, Kingston's Queen's College, and Toronto's University of Toronto, there was no shortage of either. Nor was there at the McGill Normal School.

Those seeking to improve themselves through higher learning were in the main male; a young woman was barred from becoming a doctor or a lawyer or a minister at the time. To rise in the world she could marry up. But what if the prospect of endless childbearing and child-rearing was distasteful? What if the nighttime rustlings, grunts, and moans of her parents, and the agony of her mother's birthings were a source of distaste and terror? Could a girl get out of it somehow? Could she choose another kind of fate?

*Back in Scotland, she had liked school. Liked being away from
the farmhouse and its endless chores. When the teacher rapped a cane
sharply across her little hand because she had pressed too hard on her
nib and made an ink blob, she bit her lip and blinked rather than cry.
Later, when she was no longer the youngest in the class, she liked help-
ing out. She was good at rote, mastered the times table by whispering
it to herself at night before sleep. When the teacher set her to work in
a corner with a couple of backward children, she took pride in drum-
ming into their skulls what he was unable to do.*

*She particularly liked school because while there, she was liber-
ated from her mother's firm, insistent thumb: the endless tasks – the
drawing of water at the well, the chopping of vegetables, the soaking of
nappies, the polishing of shoes, the carrying out of slops. Not that her
mother was lazy. She was just always in the family way, always worn
out, always suckling an infant, like a ewe with her lambs. Was there
a way of being a woman that did not entail such drudgery, so much
touching and being touched?*

What if she became a teacher?

Margaret Galbraith was twenty-one when her family came to the
Eastern Townships. She had probably stopped going to school in
Scotland at thirteen or fourteen, if she was lucky enough to have
gone that long. Farm children were counted on to repay their parents for their upkeep by working for the family until the age of
eighteen to twenty. A girl might then well expect to marry. Did she
have suitors? Did anyone ask how she felt about leaving her native
country? Was she bereft at abandoning the familiar, or overjoyed at
starting afresh? We can only imagine or speculate.

In Stukely she might have made a stab at playing teacher in the
village schoolhouse. It was not unusual in the summer when the
bigger boys were out in the fields, for a young woman to roll up her
sleeves and take charge. With the rowdier elements gone, keeping order was easier. Her brothers, Walter, Archibald, and Robert, fourteen,
ten, and eight respectively, might well have griped about the teacher.
During the winter, he was often a retired or cashiered soldier, or a
man incapable of worthwhile employment. Walter – chafing at the
bit and eager to help their father on the farm – might egg her on.

"C'mon, Maggie, you've always had a mind to be a teacher!"

Such "teaching" was rewarded with a bit of cash or in kind. Acquiring formal qualifications would lead to a better salary. But the one-room log cabin schoolhouse with its wood stove, hard backless benches, dog-eared mismatched textbooks, rough quill pens, rationed scraps of paper, and ample supply of birch rods was not exactly a glamorous escape hatch for a girl trying to outwit her fate.

She either picked it blindly because she needed to get away, or from a desire to help out her parents. Either out of narrow vision or because of limited options. But she picked it.

The McGill Normal School was one of three teacher-training institutions founded in 1857 for the colony of Canada East. It was intended for English-speaking Protestants, while the other two – Jacques Cartier for Montreal and Laval for Quebec – were for French Catholics. (In practice, a smattering of Catholic students also attended McGill in its early years.) Its first principal was William Dawson, recommended for the post by the governor of the colony, Sir Edmund Walker Head. A geologist, palaeontologist, author, and educator, Dawson was a brilliant polymath, born to Scottish immigrant parents in Nova Scotia and educated at the University of Edinburgh. A devout Presbyterian who once considered becoming a minister, Dawson had an enormous appetite for work and research, as well as impressive gifts as a teacher. By the time he arrived in Montreal in 1855 at the age of thirty-five, he had helped to found a provincial Normal School in Nova Scotia, and completed a monumental study of the geology of the Maritime provinces, in the course of which he discovered the earliest reptiles ever found by scientists before or since. (These findings proved crucial to Charles Darwin's conclusions about evolution, theories that the conventionally religious Dawson rejected.) Before coming to McGill, Dawson had been instrumental in the creation of the University of New Brunswick. It was there that he became acquainted with Sir Edmund Head, then the Lieutenant Governor of that colony. Head convinced McGill's Board of Governors that what they needed to guide the college was not an imported British classicist, but a scholar and scientist with an established international reputation, who just happened to have an interest in teacher training.

Though he knew next to nothing about either Montreal or McGill, Dawson accepted the offer to be the college's fifth principal, because he had just been passed over for the job he truly wanted – the chair of the natural history department of the University of Edinburgh. On his arrival he found McGill in a shambles. The college grounds were a cow pasture linked to the city by a rough trail too hazardous to attempt after nightfall. The two college buildings – today's Old Arts Building and Dawson Hall – were crumbling, and, with the exception of the medical faculty, so were the college's academic credentials.

Dawson swiftly turned the place around. Nearly a century later, Stephen Leacock wrote that McGill was "*his* work," more than any other individual's. The city's wealthy elements were won over as much by Dawson's combination of enthusiasm, high-mindedness, and courtly manners as by the fact that he had put Montreal on the map for scholarship in geology and the natural sciences. His devoutness, teetotalism, and opposition to Darwin's theories reassured a conservative establishment about the safety of entrusting young minds to his stewardship. These attributes were equally important in loosening rich purse strings to the benefit of the college.

Dawson's first important step was to accept the principalship of the Normal School, along with that of its parent institution. The idea was that by supporting teacher training, McGill would eventually admit better prepared students. Still, there appeared to be a deep suspicion of the forces that would be unleashed if the population at large were to eat from the tree of knowledge. At the inauguration ceremonies of the Normal School on March 3, 1857, Francis Fulford, the Anglican Bishop of Montreal, pronounced himself skeptical of the "blessings of increased education," since such a development would not necessarily cure the evil nature of man. On the same occasion, P. J. O. Chauveau, the Superintendent of Public Instruction of Canada East, warned mothers to be on the lookout "in case evil is spread by the teachers instead of good." Professor William Hicks of the school, however, offered a glimmer of hope for the professionalization of teachers, pointing out that up till then education had been left in the hands of the likes of disappointed clerks, who resolved "to try teaching till something better turns up" – an early formulation of the notion that those who can, do, while those who can't, teach.

By the time Margaret Galbraith stood nervously on the wooden planks of the platform of Bonaventure Station, she had jumped through a series of bureaucratic hoops. First of all she had to apply to Principal Dawson with a certificate of good moral character signed by a clergyman, along with written proof that she was at least sixteen years of age. She then faced a personal interview with the formidable Dawson in which he examined her for evidence that she could read and write and "was acquainted with the rudiments of grammar in English… arithmetic as far as the rule of three," and had "some knowledge of geography."

Once the principal issued her a certificate entitling her to proceed to the next step, she filled out a fresh application for admission in the presence of two witnesses and the Principal, all of whom had to countersign the same, before forwarding the whole lot – including all pertinent documentation – to the Superintendent of Schools. Subject to his approval, her name was inscribed in the register for 1867.

By this time, she would have made arrangements for accommodations. The specifications were ordained in the Special Regulations for the admission of Pupil-Teachers: "The pupil-teachers shall state the place of their residence, and those who cannot reside with their parents, will be permitted to live in boarding houses, but in such only as shall be specially approved of. No boarding house having permission to board male pupil-teachers, will be permitted to receive female pupil-teachers as boarders, and *vice versa*." Some exception must have been made in Margaret's case, for in the beginning she lived with the senior Notmans, who did not keep a boardinghouse.

Additional rules and regulations underlined the general expectation that pupil-teachers would be up to no good while attending the college. The institution's "Special Regulations for Government and Discipline" spelled out in no uncertain language that frequenting of taverns or gambling houses, drunkenness, keeping company with the dissolute, or "committing any act of immorality or insubordination" would lead to expulsion. The myriad possibilities for hanky-panky between students of the opposite sex – including conversation in the lecture halls – were enumerated and proscribed.

The minute attention to moral rectitude wasn't only about safeguarding the welfare of children at the hands of potentially dissolute student teachers. Pecuniary considerations also played into the general distrust of applicants. Successful applicants did not pay tuition and indeed received an allowance "of from £8 to £9," for room and board. In addition, those who like Margaret lived at a distance of more than ninety miles from Montreal, were allotted a travel allowance. For students of modest means every penny counted, and the rules were there to be obeyed.

This regime with its stringent controls bred conformity and subservience. Classes were held from nine to noon, and from one to five, Monday through Friday and on Saturday mornings. Church attendance was mandatory at least once on Sundays, but the pious would have felt the need to go more often. The course of study was so mindbogglingly extensive that it must of necessity have been superficial. Principal Dawson taught natural history and agriculture, Samson Robins arithmetic, algebra, geometry, natural philosophy, chemistry, and the art of teaching; William Hicks, history, geography, grammar, composition, moral philosophy, reading, and writing; James McGregor, the classics; James Duncan, the water colourist and lithographer, drawing; and Professor Fronteau, French. A literary society that ran to recitations and small skits was the only sanctioned creative outlet for what must have been a cowed student population.

Over the course of its fifty-year history before it morphed into the School for Teachers at Macdonald College, the Normal School would graduate nearly 3,000 students. Margaret Galbraith was not destined to be one of them.

But she did not know that. She did not suspect that she would fall prey to passion and its fruits. Could not possibly fathom that she would live a double life – attending classes diligently, cramming for exams, going home to Stukely for Christmas. She would tend to the increasingly ailing Mr. William Notman Senior until she was no longer welcome in the Notman household. She would ply her path nightly from the Normal School on Belmont Street to her lodgings and then to Robert's office on Peter Street. And then back again to her rooming house. By the fall, Robert was feeding her a stew of patent medicines. In the middle of December, she would submit to drug therapy from Dr. Patton. Later that month, she would sit for her exams and pass them with a conditional grade in maths.

Yet she would also enjoy sleigh rides in the company of another Robert, who possibly yearned for the chance to love her. She was too far gone by then – both with Robert Notman's child and her passion for him – to offer any response other than friendship.

No, when she embarked on a path to better herself, she could not know that it would be the imperatives of her own flesh that would betray her. Or that the man meeting her at the station could set her trembling at his touch and slake a thirst she had never even imagined existed. Least of all that she – who had been so repelled by the idea of childbirth – would one day desperately crave to have his child.

CHAPTER ELEVEN

Public Theatre

ONLY A SMATTERING of people witnessed the arrival of Robert Notman at the *Palais de justice* on the morning of Monday, April 20, 1868 at ten o'clock. Only those ignorant of the workings of the court or greedy for the tiniest tidbit of interest in the case saw him being placed at the bar, or heard the long, complicated, and confusing indictment. Courthouse aficionados knew that procedural matters would take up the first hour of the trial. But after the selection of the jury had been rancorously settled – it having been exceedingly difficult to put together an unbiased one – a tide of inquisitive observers swept into the chamber.

On foot, on horseback, or by carriage, they came to be entertained, shocked, and titillated. Some, perhaps many, came to glean information about the ways and means of terminating an unwanted pregnancy.

The criminal court was located on the ground floor of the east wing of the courthouse. Panelled in wood to enhance the quality of the acoustics, it had generous dimensions – sixty by forty-eight feet, and a twenty-foot-high ceiling. At the front of the room, the judge and lawyers looked like black birds of prey in their long gowns and flapping sleeves. They were the stars of the drama, at least as much as the woman at its heart, and far more so than the man whose fate hung in the balance as they speechified, wrangled, and objected. Robert Notman's voice would be heard only indirectly, when the letters he had written were read out loud, or when others cited his words; he would not himself take the stand. Rounding out the supporting cast was a wide array of witnesses, a jury, the officers of the court, and reporters scratching away furiously in their box, working to daily deadlines for the enlightenment of a larger audience.

An avid and wide-ranging audience, not just local and national, but also international. The story had already found its way back to Glasgow. On March 25, 1868 and March 28, 1868, the *Evening Post* and the *Sentinel* ran identical, if not entirely accurate pieces beneath the headline TRAGEDY IN MONTREAL – "Letters from Canada ... mention a painful case in Montreal. One Notman, a man of some position, but bad character, seduced a young woman, engaged as a teacher and much respected among her friends. At a certain stage he took her to a hotel, and brought in a doctor, who drugged and re-drugged her till she became so ill that her death seemed imminent. The doctor, alarmed, went home, and destroyed himself by a dose of prussic acid. The affair now got wind, and the friends of the lady traced up the plot to its source, and Notman was taken into custody and awaits his trial. The victim has recovered from the vile arts to which she was subjected, but as a deadly crime was effected it will go hard with Notman, for whom there was no sympathy, past or present."

Though the large outlines of the story had been common knowledge, its details remained sketchy. Those who arrived early heard the charge, the exact nature of which until then was unknown and even when presumably made explicit was so convoluted that up to and including the sequestering of the jury, it remained a puzzle to them. According to an abbreviated version published in the *Daily Witness*, Robert Notman was accused of having "on the 15th day of December, 1867, unlawfully and feloniously counseled, procured, and commanded a person named Alfred Patton, M. D., to administer a certain noxious thing to Margaret Galbraith, to procure a miscarriage." But the soup of verbiage describing the alleged crime included key words such as "intent" and "a certain noxious thing to the Jurors unknown" that would prove extremely troublesome to the unfortunate men selected to try the case. Another detail that would prove critical was the publication in the *Herald* of an incomplete version of the indictment.

As the first day of the trial wore on, it became clear that the "noxious thing" referred to was a substance called ergot of rye. A disease affecting cereals and flowering grasses – most commonly rye – ergot is caused by the parasitic fungus *Claviceps purpurea*. Humans who ingest ergot-contaminated grains suffer from ergotism, a syndrome with pathological symptoms, including burning sensations in the limbs, hallucinations, convulsions, and occasionally even death. Because affected women sometimes exhibited strong uterine contractions, an early connection was made between ergot and childbirth. From the Middle Ages on, it was observed that controlled doses could stop bleeding after childbirth. In other cases, and in different doses, ergot was linked to inducing abortion. Historically, midwives were known to employ the substance for both purposes.

By the nineteenth century respected medical doctors were also experimenting with ergot. In an issue of the *Lancet* entitled "Ergot of rye in Abortion and Hemorrhage," in June 1829, Dr. Charles Thompson detailed two case histories – giving specific information as to dosage - where it had proved effective in both the treatment of postpartum hemorrhage and of a miscarriage at twelve weeks gestation. Later in the century, Dr. John Denham, an obstetrician at the famous Dublin Lying-in Hospital and a lecturer at the Carmichael School of Medicine, surveyed both animal studies and his own large clinical practice, before concluding in 1851 that ergot did not have a deadly influence on a foetus. Quoting the research of Denham and other physicians, *The London Medical Record* of February 26, 1873 reported that "when ergot is given to a pregnant woman, even in repeated doses, any other than the full period, it produces no effect whatever beyond nausea and loss of appetite." The article reiterated the earlier finding that ergot produced no injurious effects upon a foetus *in utero* under normal circumstances. However, if administered to speed up the second stage of labour, the resulting violent contractions could prove fatal to a baby.

Of course, this study was published five years after the death of Dr. Patton and could not have a bearing on the Notman case. Still Judge Drummond's abrupt and angry ejection of women from the courtroom may well have been occasioned by a desire to deny them access to birth control information.

But even with the women and young people gone, the room remained packed with pumped up spectators. They fidgeted with impatience during the prosecutor's opening peroration. Heavy-handed, punitive, and pitiless, Thomas Kennedy Ramsay was perfectly cast as Crown attorney. He had immigrated to Canada at the age of twenty-one some twenty years earlier, a descendant of a Scottish landed family. Like all successful English-speaking jurists in Montreal, he possessed an excellent command of French. Ramsay was famous for his aggressive manner and meticulous case preparations. He lived for the law, and remained a bachelor all his life. When he was named to the bench a couple of years after the Notman case, the *Gazette* commended his erudition and pronounced him "a man of the highest character." It then added a snide if understated dig: "He has in some respects made himself unpopular."

Seeking to overwhelm by sheer volume of precedents and esoteric data, Ramsay bathed the jury in the sound of his voice. With dizzying speed, he reeled off statutes by year, number, and section, so that the reporters in the box had a great deal of trouble keeping them straight. However, all accounts tallied as to the thrust of what the prosecutor said. The case, according to Ramsay, was of the greatest public consequence and gravity. Any person who administered a poison – "a noxious thing" – or used instruments to bring on a miscarriage was guilty of a felony. The significance of the offence lay not in its outcome. It wasn't necessary to prove that "the noxious thing" was able to induce a miscarriage, or even that the woman to whom it was administered was pregnant, "about which there might exist different opinions." What was crucial was intent.

In other words, the indictment was couched in such a way that even if what Robert Notman had personally or through the agency of Dr. Patton fed Margaret was ineffectual, and even if she was not pregnant at the time, he was guilty of felony since his intention had been to frustrate nature. This intention was made explicit by the stay at the St. Lawrence Hall and the operation performed by Dr. Patton. The reason Robert Notman had to face the music alone as reported in the *Gazette* was inadvertently funny: "Dr. Patton was not produced, because two days after the commission of abortion he was found dead in his bed. ...."

Ramsay concluded his opening with the usual legal pieties about the jury making its decision based on the evidence presented in court. Jurors were to disregard what they had heard or read about the case, and put aside any feelings of sympathy they entertained for the accused. Before calling his star witness, he tried to head off the line of argument he surmised the defence would use to discredit her: "he would warn the jury against any appeals to passion; or statements... that one of the witnesses for the prosecution was also implicated. No matter if witness was as deeply implicated as prisoner, that did not affect the matter. He would now call Margaret Galbraith as the first witness."

The *Gazette* at this juncture capitalized and centred Margaret's full name. The newspaper's capitals signified the anticipatory buzz that ran through the chamber, as spectators stirred in their seats, their loins possibly also stirring. *Here comes the fallen woman, here comes the hussy, here comes Notman's whore.*

The *Morning Chronicle* gave a neat bird's eye view of the scene: "Great difficulty was experienced in bringing Miss Galbraith into court, she shrieked and fainted and at another time went into hysterics and ran out of the room. Her evidence was given in a very low tone and was repeated to the Court and Jury by Mr. Ramsay. She was very heavily veiled and manifested much agitation. Mr. Notman was very cool and collected, and watched the case closely."

The *Daily Witness* commented that Margaret showed such anguish at having to appear that she had to be "almost carried and placed in the witness box," all the while averting her veiled face from the crowd. "She was accompanied by Miss Chambers (a lady friend), who then conducted her to a large easy chair, in which she sat to give her evidence, near the jury." Both the *Daily Witness* and the *Herald* portrayed Margaret with a degree of sympathy and both made mention of the presence of Miss Chambers as Margaret's friend and companion.

As housekeeper at the St. Lawrence Hall, Letitia Chambers would testify later that day. A couple of years older than Margaret, she was also a newcomer to the city, having only arrived from Ireland in July 1867. She took a job at the St. Lawrence Hall, but – evidently intelligent and capable – she moved on quickly to more responsible management positions. Within a few years, she became the matron of the Montreal Smallpox Hospital, where she crossed paths with David McCord, an alderman with a special interest in health reform. McCord was the scion of a distinguished Montreal bilingual family of merchants, philanthropists, and art lovers. He married Letitia Chambers in 1878 over the objections of his family. (They disparaged the fact that she was a working woman. Perhaps they also remembered her participation in the Notman affair.)

As Mrs. McCord, Letitia reigned over Temple Grove, one of Montreal's grand baronial mansions. She was also fully engaged with her husband in gathering a wealth of material relating to the early history of

Canada. Their prized collection became the backbone of the McCord Museum, where, along with other treasures of Canadiana, the Notman Photographic Archives are housed today.

Of course this was all as yet in the future, but it is noteworthy that Letitia Chambers had the mettle to brave the circus in the court room at the side of the dishonoured Margaret Galbraith. It speaks to Margaret's character for being able to attract champions (there would be others over the course of the trial), and to Letitia's spunkiness – especially in light of being a newcomer and a spinster – in risking her own reputation by this association.

Though the *Gazette* gave the fullest account among all the newspapers of Margaret's entrance, it omitted mention of her companion, who sat by her side for the duration of her lengthy testimony. This was no oversight by the paper, but a deliberate glossing over the fact that a respectable woman had befriended Margaret, whom it continued to depict with the same icy hostility it had shown since the story broke.

Its reporter wrote: "A general movement was here made to see witness in this *cause celebre* [*sic*] .... [She] was accommodated with a chair within the bar immediately before the reporters box. The witness is about twenty-eight years of age, dark haired and dark eyed, with plain features. She was dressed in a dead-leaf stuff dress, with a black jacket, green gloves, bonnet, with brown veil and blue ribbons. On being asked to identify prisoner witness looked one moment at him, and then sank down in a fit, trembling in every limb."

This over-the-top entrance may have been feigned histrionics or a display of genuine hysteria. For the past eight months Margaret Galbraith had been living a double life. Its subterfuges, secret meetings, and outright lies could not have sat easily with the straitlaced morality of a doctrinaire Calvinist.

But – in light of her choice of congregation on her arrival to Montreal – that is exactly what she was. In the absence of a Presbyterian congregation in Stukely, her family had thrown in their lot with the Anglican community in pretty St. Matthew's Church, their other choice being a roving Wesleyan preacher. In joining the Coté Street Presbyterian church, Margaret proved her own orthodoxy. One of the largest Protestant congregations in the city, the Coté Street church numbered among its members both wealthy entrepreneurs and philanthropists such as sugar magnates John and Peter Redpath, and humble folk the likes of herself. It was led by the Reverend D. H. MacVicar, a stirring preacher and fervent proselytizer among local Roman Catholics and Jews, and a great endorser of missions to China. MacVicar was a dogmatic and conservative Calvinist in a period when younger Presbyterians were leaning towards a more lenient religious stance. Given Montreal's plethora of houses of worship, Margaret could have easily chosen a congregation with a softer orientation if she had been more flexible in her religious views.

As the trial opened, she was on the brink of moral and physical collapse. She had spent the past five weeks in hospital, having been discharged only two days earlier. Public scorn and ridicule compounded her private misery. Within days of the story breaking in the papers, the *Gazette* floated the rumour that she was under police surveillance, lest she flee the city. When the trial opened, both the *Herald* and Quebec's *Morning Chronicle* reported that its date had been chosen because "the principal witness for the prosecution" – Margaret – was expected to sail for Scotland by the end of the week. She appeared poised for flight, leaving Montreal being her one remaining ambition.

Following the repeated assaults on her body – both chemical and physical – and her near death experience at the hotel, she had been cast adrift by the two anchors of her life in the city. The McGill Normal School washed its hands of her on March 7. A note in the *Principal's Memoranda* dated that day stated that "Margaret Galbraith [was] reported absent since Friday Feby 21st – Since which time it is reported that she has been guilty of immoral conduct preventing her from returning." The memorandum went on to say that Margaret had been absent from gymnastic class on February 21 and from the school's regular classes since the 24th. When her professors inquired about her absence, her friend, Helen McDonald, answered on her behalf that she "was slightly unwell," with supporting evidence in the form of notes from her landlady, Mrs. Walter Wilson. Deflecting possible criticism for admitting a girl of easy virtue, the McGill memorandum explained that Miss Galbraith had entered the school with the "usual testimonials" and was understood to be an acquaintance of Mrs. Notman. At the end of the school year, McGill drafted new, stricter regulations for boarding houses.

On April 7 – a day deservedly more famous as the date of the assassination of D'Arcy McGee in Ottawa – she was thrown out of the Coté Street Presbyterian church. Her disgrace in her own eyes must have been complete when, at the monthly church meeting – the Reverend MacVicar presiding – the moderator reported "in the case of Margaret Galbraith that she acknowledged having been seduced by Robert Notman and also having by his direction taken drugs in order to procure an abortion." At the time she was still in hospital, so her fate must have been decided *in absentia*. In the notes of the meeting, the moderator wrote that "the latter part of her confession has been proven in evidence before the Criminal Court." This was technically incorrect, since the trial was yet to come, but she had given widely publicized evidence before a police magistrate. The verdict was categorical: "The session therefore resolves to remove her name from the community roll and declare her no longer a member of the church."

And now, after this crushing pronouncement and cut loose from her professional ambitions and the moorings of her faith, she had to undergo the ordeal of testifying against Robert in the fishbowl environment of a public courtroom. She would have to endure hearing every word of the incriminating letters she had kept in her lodgings under lock and key. She would have to submit to the scrutiny and mirth of those for whom her suffering and shame were a form of theatre, be it morality play or Victorian striptease in which the actors kept their clothes on while an audience of self-regarding and/or lascivious men mentally disrobed them.

But she deserved her punishment. She had sinned. The truth was she had not been seduced. She had fornicated willingly, she had burned with lust, and she had repeatedly returned to Robert's office for her forbidden pleasures. And then when God punished her with the wages of her sin, instead of shouldering her shameful responsibility, she had committed the unforgivable crime of complicity in the destruction of her baby. Robert was facing trial now because of her moral turpitude. And if she now had to pay with public disgrace, that was nothing compared to the eternal damnation awaiting her on the other side of the grave.

No wonder she succumbed to hysterics. No wonder that when Ramsay asked her the first question, she responded, "I know the prisoner," and promptly fainted. (The *Herald* editorialized pityingly, "the scene here was most painful....") After she was revived, Ramsay inquired how long she had known the prisoner. Margaret threw her hands in the air, flung herself backwards, and burst into tears.

There now began the acrimonious skirmishing between prosecution and defence that Ramsay had anticipated.

A firebrand of the Montreal Irish community, chief defence counsel Bernard Devlin was the complete foil to Ramsay's dour persona. He wasn't shy about voicing his opinions against the union of England and Ireland, served frequently as president of the St. Patrick's Society, and had in a recent hotly contested election campaign in Montreal West been alleged to be a Fenian sympathizer. (Devlin lost to D'Arcy McGee.)

A decade earlier, Devlin and Lewis Thomas Drummond – in the days before he was called to the bench – had teamed up to defend Francis Tumblety, an American quack arrested in Montreal on charges of attempting to abort a city prostitute. This old association between the two Irishmen in no way softened Drummond's stance towards the defence. If anything, it made him even more bloody-minded.

Devlin partnered up with William Warren Hastings Kerr in the Notman case. Kerr was one of the few players in the drama to be a native Canadian. Born in Trois-Rivières in 1826 and educated in Quebec City and in Kingston, he settled in Montreal, and eventually became Dean of Law at McGill University. Naturally pugnacious, Kerr immediately went on the offensive. He accused Miss Galbraith of being a principal offender in the case. Someone should warn her about the possibility of incriminating herself. Had she not consented to taking the drug in question? He argued that according to an earlier statute it would have been possible to indict her as aiding and abetting in the act. Judge Drummond nipped this line of argument in the bud instantly, and Ramsay resumed his examination by repeating his question about the length of her acquaintanceship with Notman.

"I have known the prisoner seven or eight months."

When the prosecutor introduced the subject of Dr. Patton, Margaret gave a reticent response. ·

"I have seen Dr. Patton."

Would that have been Dr. Alfred Patton?

"I do not know his Christian name."

When had she met the doctor for the first time?

"I first saw him about the 15th of December."

And where had this meeting taken place?"

"It was in Mr. Notman's office, in St. Peter Street. . . . This was a few days before the Christmas holidays. I met him there by appointment."

Ramsay asked who had made this appointment, eliciting an objection from Bernard Devlin. Since Miss Galbraith had not been present when the appointment was made, she should not answer. The judge overruled the objection, but Devlin insisted on repeating it. Irritated, Judge Drummond said that he had already ruled, but would put the question to the witness himself. Devlin asked to have his objection written into the record.

In answer to the judge's question, Margaret said, "Mr. Notman requested me to meet him there."

Ramsay resumed his role as questioner and requested that she describe what happened next.

"There was no one at the office when I went. It was about half-past two in the afternoon. About half an hour afterwards a gentleman came in whom I supposed to be Dr. Patton."

A key question: Why had this appointment been made?

There was a long pause, during which Margaret covered her face. "I went there because I wished to ask his advice." Ramsay coaxed her along. "I went to get some medicine from him." But why did she need medicine? "I did not know what was the matter with me, and I went to ask Dr. Patton what ailed me."

Really? She had no idea what was wrong with her? "I thought I was pregnant." And then? "I underwent an examination, and he gave me some medicine."

"Did he tell you what that medicine was?"

Kerr, of the defence, had had enough. He burst out an objection that any answer to this question would be hearsay. "Acts can be given in evidence, not in words. This is making words into deeds."

Ramsay stated that in order to understand the prisoner's intent, it was necessary to determine Dr. Patton's as well.

Devlin interjected that this line of questioning was injurious to his client. He challenged the prosecutor to cite a single precedent for the admission of this type of evidence.

For once the judge sustained an objection from the defence.

Unfazed, Ramsay resumed his step-by-step questioning: did the doctor give her medicine, was it before or after he had examined her, what was it for, when did she take it?

"He gave me a bottle of medicine…. I took some of it. He gave it to me in the office."

Was the bottle labelled in any way?

"The bottle had no label…. It was after he had examined me that he gave me this medicine." (Much would be made later on about the lack of a label on the bottle, the implication being that the doctor was hiding the nature of its contents.)

What did the doctor know of her condition?

"I don't remember what I told Dr. Patton. I think I told him what I thought was the matter with me. He examined me after I had spoken to him."

When Ramsay asked if the prisoner knew of her problem, he got a surprisingly spirited response. "I think the prisoner knew, at least he ought to have known what was the matter with me. I know I told him that I thought I was pregnant."

An exchange here occurred between Ramsay and Devlin that the *Gazette* described as "a pleasant spar." Devlin accused Ramsay of leading the witness. The paper then gleefully noted that "Mr. Devlin was worsted."

Ramsay began closing in. When she told Notman that she thought she was pregnant, had he given her any sort of medicine?

"He had previously given me something of this kind upon some conversation of this sort. It was some pills, also a small phial of liquid."

Here Adolphe Bissonette, the High Constable, was called to the witness stand. After identifying himself, he produced a small empty bottle which he said he had received from Mr. Ramsay on March 25 at the courthouse. He testified to passing the vial the following day to Dr. Gilbert Girdwood for microscopic analysis, and having it returned to him by the doctor two days later.

Ramsay zeroed in on the item of evidence. Had Miss Galbraith seen it before? " This is the bottle which I got from Dr. Patton. It was about half full when I got it from Dr. Patton. I gave it to [you] Mr. Ramsay on the 25th March at the English General Hospital."

This was the first mention of Margaret being hospitalized at the Montreal General Hospital, an indication of just how ill she had been. Hospitals of the time were abodes of death.

What had the bottle contained?

"I believe it contained ergot of rye."

Had she tampered with it in any way?

"I put nothing into the phial. The bottle is in the same condition as when I gave it to you."

Had it been full, was it a powder or a liquid inside?

"The bottle was about half full when Dr. Patton gave it to me.... The bottle contained a powder."

Ramsay changed tack. Had the prisoner been present at her appointment with Dr. Patton?

"On the occasion of my meeting Dr. Patton, on 15 December, at the prisoner's office, the prisoner was not in town. He had been absent from town two or three days."

In that case, how did she know to meet Dr. Patton?

"The prisoner... told me the day previous to his going away to meet Dr. Patton in his (prisoner's) office."

Before that time, had she been in touch with Dr. Patton by means of the prisoner?

"I did not communicate with Dr. Patton, through the prisoner, previous to 15 December."

Had she corresponded with Notman while he was gone?

"I sent letters to the prisoner while he was out of town, and I received answers. I, too, was out of town during the two weeks of the Christmas holidays. I left town on the 19th or 20th of December and returned on the ninth or 10th of January."

Had she conversed with the prisoner about her pregnancy once they were both in town?

"When I returned from the country I had some conversation with the prisoner respecting my supposed condition of pregnancy."

When would this have been?

"It was some time in January. I told the prisoner that I had got some medicine from Dr. Patton, but that it had not had, as I supposed, the desired effect. He asked if I had taken it, and I replied that I had."

What had she meant by those words "the desired effect"?

"By the desired effect, I meant the procuring of miscarriage."

And what had been the prisoner's response?

Margaret took a deep breath and held it. The silence of the room was almost palpable, as she pronounced some of the most damning words in the entire trial.

"The prisoner answered that he would himself see Dr. Patton, and he also said he would leave nothing undone that could be done."

There was a general hubbub. Kerr jumped to his feet and began objecting. The reporters scribbled in furious shorthand that there was another skirmish between learned counsel in which Mr. Ramsay succeeded in carrying his point.

Under cover of the din, Margaret turned pleading eyes towards Letitia Chambers. Her face through the brown veil was etched with fatigue, her shoulders in the black jacket slumped.

"What time is it, Miss Chambers? Surely it is time for the recess?"

Surreptitiously Letitia reached for the pocket watch tucked with its chain into her waistband. "It is not yet even noon, Miss Galbraith," she whispered. "We shall not break yet for another hour at least."

"I don't know that I can last..."

Letitia slipped the watch back into its groove, and gave a quick clandestine squeeze to Margaret's fingers. "You must."

For another hour and a half, they continued to badger her with their unrelenting questions. She knew now that she must not succumb to hysterics; she would not escape until she answered every last one of them. And in between, there were the repeated squabbles between these learned men. And then once again they turned their attention to her and she must concentrate on keeping her facts very straight. Who had been in the inner office, who in the outer? Which month was that in, January, February? What date in February? Then another point from the defence trying to bolster Robert's case. Oh, how badly she wanted it to go well with Robert. But it did not appear to be going well.

She must not think about Robert now! A question was being hurled at her again, and another one. A phrase began to buzz through her head: "They compassed me about like bees... they compassed me about like bees..." Where was that from? From the Gospels? From the prophets? No, no, no – she must keep her mind on the matter now. She must answer the question. She must answer the question in full sentences, the way Mr. Ramsay had instructed her. It was not hard to do that, she knew she could do that. She was a clever girl, she could do it, it was just the way you had to do in school. It was what she herself would have taught in school, had she not sinned, had she not sinned and forever cast herself out of that Garden of Eden in which she might have once become a teacher.

She forced herself to concentrate on Ramsay's thin lips beneath the shag of his moustache.

What did she think the prisoner meant when he said "he would leave nothing undone that could be done"? What more could be done?

"I imagined that Dr. Patton, as a medical man, could do something more than giving me medicine to procure a miscarriage."

When had she and the prisoner discussed this possibility?

Bernard Devlin rose indignantly and said that the indictment specifically charged the prisoner with complicity in an act committed on December 15. The prosecution must limit itself. Judge Drummond overruled him and instructed the witness to continue.

"After my return from the country I had a conversation with the prisoner on the subject ...

When had this been?, asked the prosecutor.

"I can't remember the time ..."

She should try ...

"It was in January, before I went to the St. Lawrence Hall."

Devlin repeated his objection that conversations occurring in January could not apply to a crime supposed to have taken place on December 15. The judge again reiterated that *any* conversation – both before and after the time specified in the indictment – was perfectly admissible if it shed light on the prisoner's intent.

Ramsay continued to worry away at his bone. Had she and the prisoner continued to discuss what Dr. Patton might be able to do for her, and if so where and when had they conversed about it?

"I and the prisoner had a conversation in the prisoner's office some time in February. I went to St. Lawrence Hall on a Saturday – I think it was on the 22nd February.... On that Saturday I conversed with him on the subject before I went to the Hall.

Devlin voiced his objection for the third time to a line of examination so long after the date on which the alleged offence was said to have been committed. Yet again the judge overruled him and urged the witness to continue.

"I told the prisoner in the course of our conversation on the 22nd February, that I was not well, and that I should like to see Dr. Patton. He then sent for Dr. Patton, who came there, in a short time. I remained there along with the prisoner, and I think we were both of us present when Dr. Patton arrived. The prisoner was in the outer office, while I was in the inner office, with Dr. Patton."

At 1:15 the longed-for recess was called. The court had been in session for more than three hours, but it was clear that the most crucial parts of Margaret Galbraith's testimony were yet to come.

1. Robert Notman, Montreal, 1863
An enigmatic anti-hero.

I-7321.1 © McCord Museum

2. Miss Galbraith, Montreal, 1868
Did she have "a fatal tendency to espouse a losing cause"?

I-29865.1 © McCord Museum

3. Mr. Benning, Montreal, 1868
He may have had an anxiety disorder.

4. Dr. Robert Palmer Howard, Montreal, 1865
According to William Osler, he "combined a
stern sense of duty with the mental freshness of youth."

I-16893.1 © McCord Museum

5. Dr. Craik, Montreal, 1865
He began the postmortem "without the least idea of the cause of death."

I-19016.1 © McCord Museum

6. F. W. L. Penton, Montreal, 1863
Though chronically understaffed, the chief of
police found a culprit and made a case.

I-9553.1 © McCord Museum

7. William Notman, Montreal, 1862
Failure and discredit brought him to the shores of the St. Lawrence.

I-4443.1 © McCord Museum

8. Mrs. William Notman, Montreal, 1862
Her husband only ever referred to her as "dear Alice."

I-4486.1 © McCord Museum

9. Mrs. Ramsay, Montreal, 1861
"Mrs R received me as if I had been a dear sister,"
Alice wrote to her mother back home.

I-1176 © McCord Museum

10. Missie Fanny Notman, Montreal, 1861
Winsome ways and a tragic end.

I-1873.1 © McCord Museum

11. "The Newsboy", William McF. Notman, Montreal, 1866
Brought up in the studio and later a fine photographer in his own right.

I-19926 © McCord Museum

12. Mrs. Robert Notman, Montreal, 1863
Annie Birks: stunned eyes and a rigid back.

I-8051.1 © McCord Museum

13. Annie Notman, Montreal, 1869
Little Annie, a cherished member of the Notman clan.

I-39722.1 © McCord Museum

14. Court House, Notre Dame Street, Montreal, 1859
The city's most impressive public building.

N-0000.193.29.1 © McCord Museum

15. Painted photograph of Honourable Judge L. T. Drummond,
A brilliant man of many parts and perplexing contradictions.

II-67733.0.1 © McCord Museum

16. Thomas Kennedy Ramsay, Montreal, 1870
Punitive and pitiless, he was perfectly cast as prosecutor.

I-43819.1 © McCord Museum

17. Bernard Devlin, Montreal, 1874
The chief defence counsel was an eloquent firebrand.

II-5076.0 © McCord Museum

18. Miss Letitia Chambers, Montreal, 1876
The lowly housekeeper of the St. Lawrence Hall would one day reign
over one of Montreal's great mansions.

II-41898.1 © McCord Museum

19. Doctor Patton, Montreal, 1862
Why had he lost his nerve?

I-3718.1 © McCord Museum

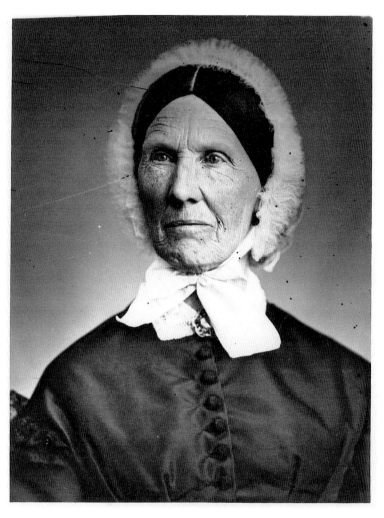

20. Mrs. Walter Wilson, Montreal, 1866
Despite her stern appearance, she had a kind heart.

I-21355 © McCord Museum

21. St. Lawrence Hall, St. James Street, Montreal, about 1890
Montreal's finest hotel and a haven for Confederate spies.

VIEW-1876 © McCord Museum

22. Henry Hogan, Montreal, 1870
Affable and shrewd, the proprietor of the St. Lawrence Hall
retained a soft spot for Lincoln's assassin.

I-46751.1 © McCord Museum

23. Miss Annie Notman, Montreal, 1882
She worked at the Notman studio and could see through
a camera's tricks.

II-66977.1 © McCord Museum

24. William Notman and sons Charles, George and William McF.,
Montreal, 1890
Father and sons documented the new Dominion's cities and
countryside, its citizens at work and play.

II-93256 © McCord Museum

The Ghost of Dr. Patton

AFTER RECESS, Miss Chambers once more settled Margaret into her armchair in front of the judge and then seated herself at her friend's side. As Ramsay recommenced his methodical questioning, it became progressively clearer that he was constructing his case as if peeling an onion. The outer skin was the examination of the girl. Then, layer upon layer, as the tension in the courtroom heightened with each passing minute, he introduced incriminating written, medical, and forensic evidence.

Margaret asked herself what road had brought her to this pass, the object of these inquisitive and appraising eyes, these lewd and censorious insinuations, these titters of opprobrium. And then as, bit by bit, Mr. Ramsay, then Mr. Devlin, pulled the story out her – as if they were pulling out her very entrails – in her mind's eye she pictured a path marked out by a trail of breadcrumbs scattered as in an ill-omened fairytale. Each crumb represented an instant of carnal pleasure and its payment in days and weeks of anguish. There were other ever tinier specks along the trail. They stood for hope and for dashed hopes.

And even as these thoughts passed through her mind, she recited her story haltingly but with the composure that had eluded her earlier in the day. Over recess she had resolved not to succumb again to hysterics. Nothing would be gained by it: she remembered what her friend Robert Murray had said to her when they discussed the trial while she was in hospital. She must try to tell the truth and tell it straight. It was the only way.

And so, in answer to Mr. Ramsay, she described how on Saturday February 22 she had gone to the prisoner's office to see Dr. Patton. Notman's office on Peter Street consisted of two rooms. The doctor examined her in the inner chamber and then proceeded to the outer room to confer with Robert. She did not have to explain the purpose of this physical examination to the court. The doctor must have been trying to determine if by some fluke the various means tried until then to abort her had been successful. After the private conversation between the two men, Notman informed her that he would rent rooms for her in the St. Lawrence Hall, where a "miscarriage" would take place. She then returned to her new lodgings on Lagauchetiere Street to pack up her necessities.

The court would not hear about Robert's activities until the following day's session, but according to Charles St. Jacques, assistant bookkeeper at the St. Lawrence Hall who testified on the second day of the trial, Robert Notman made a reservation for a so-called "Miss Williams" from South Stukely, on the afternoon of February 22 around four o'clock. Notman claimed that the lady would arrive by local train later that day. Notman chose a two-room suite consisting of a sitting room and adjoining bedroom, both of which opened onto the corridor by the hotel's Craig Street entrance. He signed the register on behalf of the lady, and later that afternoon confirmed her arrival with the clerk. While St. Jacques observed Notman coming and going to and from the suite frequently over the course of the next few days, he never laid eyes on "Miss Williams."

Margaret told the court that she met Robert at the hotel at seven. The doctor arrived a couple of hours later and stayed all night. Grilled about what he had actually done to her, Margaret at first responded, "I don't know what he did. I was very sick, and he waited upon me." When prodded further, she gave an evasive answer: "Dr. Patton did no more than any other medical man would have done under the circumstances." The upshot of Patton's ministrations was the desired miscarriage, she said. For such an outcome, Ramsay argued, Dr. Patton must have used "means" – instruments. Margaret denied this strenuously and dropped a bombshell at the same time. "He made use of the sponge-tents some days before at the prisoner's office. Mr. Notman was present at the time."

An aggressive remedy for severe menstrual cramps, sponge tents were cervical dilators. Made of thin, cone-shaped pieces of compressed sponge designed to enlarge the opening of the uterus, their use often resulted in rampant infections. The image of Margaret lying on a desk in Notman's office, legs splayed – perhaps held down by her lover – skirts bunched around her waist, the doctor forcing sponges into her secret place floated before the eyes of the courtroom.

The revelations continued. After the ordeal of the delivery of the foetus in the wee hours of Sunday, she had not been able to get out of bed until Monday morning, and then only for a couple of hours. It was the same story on Tuesday. During this time she saw no one but Notman and Dr. Patton, and on one occasion a chambermaid; she could not remember whether this visit was on Sunday or Monday. By Wednesday she was so ill she could not get out of bed. The doctor came for the last time at eleven that night. "I was then in bed, and suffering."

As Margaret recited her testimony step by painful step, the dimensions of the tragedy and its underlying irony became starkly apparent to even the dullest spectator. Yes, Margaret Galbraith was ruined. Yes, Robert Notman had ruined her. But the disgraced lovers were alive to face the consequences of their actions. Yet a ghostly void hovered over the chamber. Thoughts of the very dead Dr. Patton could not have been far from the minds of those present. His name, pronounced over and over again, reverberated like a gong that resounds long after it has been struck.

Over the course of the afternoon it became ever more obvious that for months Notman and Dr. Patton – with the full co-operation of the patient – had subjected her to a variety of torments designed to end her pregnancy and that these measures must inevitably have seriously compromised her health.

What could have possessed Alfred Patton to overcome his scruples and breach the code of his profession? Was it friendship with Robert? Was it pity for the girl? Was it greed? But if any or all of these motives, why had he lost his nerve?

Within a few days of Patton's suicide, these questions were already being publicly debated. On March 8 the Reverend Dr. Irvine of the Knox Presbyterian Church on Dorchester Street at Mansfield preached an eloquent sermon on the text "Be sure your sin will find you out." While admitting that he didn't know Dr. Patton personally, Dr. Irvine revealed that he was acquainted with Dr. Patton's family in Ireland ("some of whom I know to be among the excellent of the earth"). He could also vouch that Alfred's older brother was a minister "of superior gifts and eminent piety." Dr. Irvine could not reconcile what he knew of Dr. Patton with the idea that he had been motivated by love of money. Perhaps the doctor had been moved by "the impulses of an over-generous nature to aid guilty parties in their attempts to conceal sin and screen themselves from the shame of exposure…." Dr. Patton had a reputation as "an estimable and sympathizing man" and there was evidence that he "had been indulging in the use of ardent spirits." Perhaps in a weak moment he had agreed "to undertake the wicked task which had ended so fatally." In the final analysis, Dr. Irvine judged the doctor's suicide an act of remorse and despair, a "sad and painful" event that had stunned a whole community and had the unintentional and ironic twist of exposing "the sin he was laboring to conceal."

Dr. Irvine's characterization of Dr. Patton may not have been far off the mark. Alfred Patton was born into a prosperous Anglo-Irish family around 1840, in a suburb of Belfast called Ballymacarrett. At a young age he took to the sea as a ship's surgeon and had been plying the Atlantic between Liverpool and Montreal at least since 1862, when he was photographed at the Notman Studio. In April 1863, when the S.S. *Anglo Saxon* ran aground in a storm off the coast of Newfoundland, he acted heroically during a horrific shipwreck. With the help of other crew, Patton managed to save the lives of eighty-three women and children, while 237 unfortunates perished.

As came to light at the inquest into his death, Dr. Patton's relationship with both friends and patients tended to involve alcohol. But, then as now, having a social drink or two was not out of line for an outgoing and convivial young man. With many acquaintances, he had also had discussions about the financial prospects of his practice. But this too was a normal preoccupation for someone who had just hung up his shingle.

Was he friends with Robert? The *Glasgow Times* may or may not have been in the know when, several months after the fact, it observed that "the Montreal papers chronicle the suicide of a Dr. Patton, a young medical man who had been accused of malpractice as respects a girl whom a friend had seduced."

Had he been sucked into the plight of the lovers almost inadvertently? He and Robert, two single men in their cups – one a fine bachelor, the other a widower on the make – hatched a plan that went deadly awry, with events spiralling out of control. If he had kept his head for a few more hours, not a whiff of the story would have escaped. But it would have been hard for him to keep his head. As we shall see, the staff of the St. Lawrence Hall were becoming suspicious about the goings-on in rooms 103 and 104. For days on end, this upscale establishment had been harbouring a missing girl. If rumours were not already circulating, they would have been soon. After days of loss of blood, and months of unrelenting stress, the girl was in pain and her vital signs were flagging. To ease her suffering, he had administered morphine again earlier that day, and when he returned at night she was so weak that he believed he had lost her.

In the courtroom Ramsay now backtracked in order to introduce the notorious letters whose existence and damning nature had been long ballyhooed in the press. High Constable Bissonette was sworn in and produced eleven letters, saying that he had received them from the chief of police on March 11. Margaret recounted how she had lied on Saturday evening to Mrs. Wilson, her new landlady on Lagauchetiere Street, telling her that she was off to keep the recently widowed Mrs. Notman Senior company. She had packed a little valise with books and sundry small personal items for the projected overnight stay at the hotel. It was a touching detail: despite all that she had been through in the past few months, she was naïve enough to hope for a short, smooth convalescence whiled away with literature.

Back on Lagauchetiere Street, she left behind a locked trunk in her bedroom. It contained the letters that Robert had sent her over the course of several weeks.

The High Constable handed over a small bundle of papers to Mr. Ramsay, who – puffed up with self-importance – placed them in Margaret's hands and urged her to inspect them carefully. Margaret identified Robert's writing, and, in answer to Ramsay's questions, tried to put them in context. Some of the letters had arrived by post, she said, others were hand-delivered by a boy, some alluded to conversations between her and Robert, others to meetings between them, and the letter of December 21 referred to her appointment with Dr. Patton on December 15. Yes, she said, these were the only letters she ever received from Robert; yes, she possessed keys to his office.

The letters were then read out loud. The *Gazette* summarized them derisively in its report the next day; the *Daily Witness* more objectively. The *Herald* printed nine of the stated eleven, a decision that would prove fateful in the larger story of Robert Notman's life.

1.

Montreal, 31st October, '67

Dear Mag, – I went home [his parents' house on Eliot Terrace] early last night with the intention of being down at 8 as arranged, and left the gas burning and a good fire on [at the office on Peter Street], but feeling a little drowsy when reading the evening papers I thought I would take a nap for half an hour as it was only 7. When I woke up I found it was 9.30. I made a rush to the place but found you had gone. After putting the gas out I started home smoking my pipe, being the only thing I had to console me. Come round at 5 p.m. if you can, if you don't come at 5, I will expect you at 8, when I will be sure to be there. Hoping the other matter is all right.

Yours very truly,

R. Notman

2.

Montreal, 4th Nov, '67

Dear Mag, – Call as you go home at 5. I have a parcel for you.

Yours truly,

R. Notman

3.

New York, 29th Nov., 1867

Dear Mag, – I intended writing you from Boston, but had not time. I find I won't be able to get them till Tuesday [Dec 3] morning. I would like you to come round on Tuesday at five. I hope that little arrangement is all right. I have been a very good boy since I left home. Excuse haste,

with very kind love,
     Yours truly,
     R. Notman

                    4.

[undated]
     Dear Mag, – I left the key again inside the door, please give the boy the small keys. How do you feel this morning? I shall have all ready for you at 5.
     Yours truly.
     R. Notman

7 45 A.M.

                    5.

[undated]
     Dear Mag –
     As usual, I fell sound asleep last night, and only awoke at 11. I did not come down there, as I was sure you had gone. I expected to see you in the morning after what you told me last night. The doctor has just been in, and is anxious to hear how you are. He says he was down last night about 8:30, and no one was there. What time will I expect you to-day, and how do you feel now?
     Yours truly,
     Robert Notman

                    6.

QUEEN'S HOTEL, TORONTO, 18th December, 1867
     Dear Mag, –
     I only arrived here last night, when I rec'd your letter, which made me feel very bad, as I would rather that affair had not been done. However, I hope it has given the desired effect, and that you will go home [for Christmas

to Stukely] lighter in both *body* and mind. I have got rid of my cold, and have been very successful in business. Write me on receipt of this, as I am very anxious (to the same address.)... I wish I was in Montreal, so that I could see you off comfortably [on the train]. Send me the address of your father's place, as I can't find the book it is in. With kind love, dear Mag, and lots of kisses,

Yours truly,
R. Notman

7.

Montreal, 21ˢᵗ Dec. 1867
Dear Mag, On my arrival this morning, I called at once on Dr. Paton [*sic*], and recd your letter. You have no idea how much I think of your troubles. However, we must hope for the best, and from what the Dr. told me to-day, I am sure it is all right. I shall be anxious till I hear from you again. Address as before to the Queen's Hotel, Toronto, as I leave again tonight, and only arrived at 2 this morning, so as to be at poor Father's funeral [William Notman Senior died "of paralysis" on December 19]. Mother is very poorly, I am afraid she won't be long after him. I should have been at the house by this time, you must excuse me closing this so hurriedly. With kind love, and lots of kisses. Hoping to hear good news.

Yours very truly,
R. Notman
Telegraph either the Dr. or me if necessary.
R.N.

8.

HAMILTON, 27ᵗʰ Dec. 1867.
Dearest Mag, – Yours of the 23ʳᵈ has just been forwarded to me. I wrote you on Saturday last from Montreal, and you don't mention having recd it. Unless you have left

any of my letters lying about, it is impossible that any one should know about you and I corresponding. I really don't know what to say about the other matter, and can't understand, after all that has been done, how it can continue so. I intend spending New Year's at St. Mary's [home of his sister Maggie, wife of Dr. David Harrison], and will see what Dr. Harrison would advise, and will write you at once. I intend leaving for London tomorrow and then I have St. Mary's, Toronto, Belleville and Brockville to go to, so it will be the 10th before I get home. When do you intend returning to Montreal. I shall not write again to Stukely until I hear from you, in case you have left. I would give a good deal if I could have a chat with you, as I feel very anxious, but you must bear up as well as you can. There is no doubt it will be all right, but merely wants time, as I can't see how it can go after what had passed. It is a most unfortunate affair altogether, and if there was anything more could be done, whatever it cost me, you know I would do it. My opinion is that when you come in to town it should be probed again, as I explained to you already that it was better to wait for that operation. However I shall have a talk with Dr. Harrison, and will write, but if you want me to come home I will do so at once. And now, my dear Mag, cheer up, I will leave nothing undone that can be done. With kind love, lots of kisses and the compliments of the season,

Yours very truly,

R. Notman

P.S. – On receipt of this address Queen's Hotel, Toronto, [write] and I will get it.

R.N.

9.

Toronto, 6th Jan. '68

Dear Mag, – I have only time to acknowledge receipt of your two letters. I am glad to hear you have left Miss Tannock's. I shall be home on Wednesday night [8 January].

Call at the place between 12 and 1, or 5 and 6 on Thursday whichever is most convenient. Don't have anything done till I come home,

    Yours very truly,

    R. Notman

As the letters were read out loud, the mentions of "Mag," and the kisses being sent her way elicited snickers in the courtroom. The reference to Robert being a very good boy while in New York was found to be particularly hilarious. In the next day's *Gazette*, the reporter sneered that Robert appeared "generally to have fallen asleep and disappointed her when[ever] he made an engagement with her." The more dispassionate *Daily Witness* described the correspondence as "frequently of a trivial nature." That was true, but beneath the episodic account of the minutiae of everyday life stretched the bare bones of a woman's desperate desire to preserve her reputation. Recognition of this fact quickly sobered the atmosphere in the chamber. So too did the allusion to leaving nothing undone that could be done – words that echoed that morning's testimony – and to probes, an "operation," and a procedure that Robert wished "had not been done." There could be no doubt of the couple's blatant intent to terminate the pregnancy.

The letters in fact are an oblique account of the lovers' history from the end of October 1867 to the end of the Christmas break of 1867-1868. While in town, Robert seemed to drift between idling, dozing, and forgetfulness. At the same time, he was running a successful import and wholesale business in photographic supplies that required frequent, almost frenetic travel. The couple's trysting place was his office, and possibly Margaret's habit of traipsing back and forth between it and her rooming house had made her *persona non grata* with her landlady, Mrs. Tannock. As a result, she had had to search for new lodgings. (Discovery of the affair by Mrs. Notman Senior almost certainly accounted for her earlier dismissal from the Notman household.)

Right from the beginning of the correspondence, there is a curious dichotomy in Robert's attitude to Margaret. On the one hand, his lack of interest is so obvious I want to scream at her across the void of time between us a sentence made famous by an episode of the television series *Sex in the City:* "He's just not that into you!" But, on the other hand, he was undoubtedly concerned about her welfare and trying to ease her condition both, as he wrote, "in *body and mind.*" From the outset of the suspected pregnancy, he was provisioning her with products that he hoped would do the trick – perhaps those ubiquitous Moffat's Life Pills, Spalding's Cephalic Pills, Dr. Holloway's Pills, or Dr. Radway's Pills so readily advertised in the city's English papers. He hired one doctor, and planned to consult his brother-in-law, Dr. Harrison in St. Mary's, while on his travels (a strategy of dubious judgment). He was true to his word that he would not spare any cost to help her out and would lead nothing undone that could be done. He spent lavishly to put her up in comfort.

This was the enigma of Robert Notman. He was not an out-and-out scoundrel, who washed his hands of a discarded mistress. But neither was he an honourable man, for an honourable man would have married her. As Judge Drummond later pointed out, the negligible class difference between them was far outweighed by the girl's beauty, intelligence, and grace under pressure. More than likely his parents with whom he lived and who were probably raising little Annie, opposed any union with a servant girl they had sacked. Yet a man of character – after all, he was thirty-one and not a callow boy – would have stood up to the pressure.

After the letters were tabled, Ramsay asked Margaret to summarize the order of events, before handing her over to Devlin for cross-examination. She recapped for the court that she first met Robert at his mother's, where she was a servant for four months. In September, she moved to Mrs. Tannock's, and after Christmas to Mrs. Wilson's. Then she returned home for the Christmas break. Upon being asked about when she became pregnant, she responded, "I have no doubt I was pregnant during the months of December, January, and February."

This was a piece of adroit phrasing; Margaret may not have had any doubts about being pregnant in December, January, and February, but she was already fearful of being with child by the end of

October, when Robert wrote that he hoped "the other matter is all right." A few days later, he had a parcel for her, and by the end of November, he was optimistic that the "little arrangement is all right." Fudging the details of the pregnancy was crucial, since the law was much harsher towards the procurer of a late-term abortion.

Prosecutor Ramsay took his seat and Bernard Devlin stood to cross-examine the witness. Because he was unprepared to put his client on the stand, Devlin strove to demonstrate Robert's innocence by proving that he was out of town at the time of the alleged crime on December 15. In response to his questions, Margaret replied that Notman had left Montreal for Toronto around December 12, had been away until he returned to attend his father's funeral, and that they had not spoken with each other in that interval. When pressed, she said that the medical treatment that she received from Dr. Patton was at her own request. No, he had not been present when the doctor gave her the bottle of medicine. She denied that the prisoner had ever visited her at Mrs. Wilson's.

A great deal of time was now spent in establishing that she had placed the bottle of medicine in her trunk at the Wilsons'. The trunk was also where she had kept Robert's letters until he was arrested. She testified that she always kept the trunk locked, and that was the state in which she left it when she departed for the hotel on February 22. When she was hospitalized at what she called the English Hospital – the Montreal General – the trunk was brought to her. To her shock and dismay, the lock had been forced and the hinges broken off. She had no idea by whom. She was uncertain whether the vial of medicine had been tampered with in the meantime, but it was her impression that it looked the same now as when she first obtained it. No, she had never shown the bottle to anyone after she received it from Dr. Patton.

The prosecutor once more exchanged places with the defence counsel. For no clear reason, Ramsay asked about Margaret's marital status. It must have been painful to pronounce the words, "I am unmarried."

But the nadir of humiliations was yet to come. Dr. Francis Wayland Campbell was called and sworn in. An exact contemporary of Robert Notman, Dr. Campbell was a rising star of the Montreal medical establishment, and a many sided man. The son of Rollo Campbell, a Scottish immigrant who made his mark in the city as publisher of the 1840s Reform newspaper the *Montreal Pilot*, Francis Campbell was born in the city in 1837 and as a teenager worked for several years at his father's paper. He also took an interest in the military, and participated in volunteer militia units that repelled Fenian attacks in 1866 and in 1870.

Campbell studied medicine first at McGill and then in Europe, and subsequently set up a practice in his hometown in 1862. A couple of years later he and surgeon George Edgeworth Fenwick co-founded the *Canada Medical Journal*, a well-regarded medical periodical. Three years after the Notman trial, Campbell would be instrumental in the establishment of a new medical school in Montreal in competition with McGill, that would become the medical faculty of Bishop's College. A Freemason, he was a progressive thinker who championed the admission of women to Bishop's – the first institution in Quebec to accept females wanting to be doctors.

In an afternoon of sensational revelations, Dr. Campbell's vivid testimony was unparalleled for grossness. He testified that at three o'clock on the afternoon of Thursday, February 27, a messenger boy from the St. Lawrence Hall had called on him, asking him to attend an emergency at Room 103 of the hotel. The boy would not say who had sent him. When he arrived at the hotel, Mr. Hogan, its proprietor, requested an interview with him after he had seen his patient. Mr. Notman answered his knock at the door and informed him that there was a sick lady in the adjacent Room 104, who had been attended up till now by Dr. Patton, but whose care he now wished to assign to him.

"I asked him why Dr. Patton had ceased his attendance and was told he had been found dead in his bed that [morning]; that was my first knowledge of Dr. Patton's death. I inquired what was the matter with the lady, and was referred to the lady herself for information. The door leading into 104 was opened by someone, and I was shown in. I there saw ... Miss Galbraith in bed. She told me she had a miscarriage on the previous Sunday morning. She said Dr. Patton had attended her. I found her exceedingly ill, looking very pale, the eyes were considerably sunken, and her pulse was about 120. [Also there was] considerable fever present. Her tongue was coated with a yellow pile;... there was a slight tenderness over the abdomen, and I drew off about a pint and a half of strongly foetid urine. I then made a more particular examination and found external organs swollen and congested, ... white lines running from groin to thigh. ... There was enlargement of the nipples [and] discolouration of *areola*, and glandular enlargement; there was also a profuse lochial discharge. The breasts were much swollen and hard, and contained milk; and there was enlargement of the nipples. All these signs along with others showed the patient had been pregnant and recently delivered of a child, say in the fourth or fifth month. After I had given some general instructions, I found the prisoner and told him the patient was so ill that she must have a nurse to wait upon her, and he asked me to get one. I then went into the office where I saw Mr. Hogan, with whom I had some conversation. I returned at six, when I found Miss Chambers, the housekeeper, in the room; I gave her what directions I thought necessary. I left, and returned at ten that night. I sent her a nurse next day, and continued to attend her for a week or more."

It is not clear whether Margaret was still in the courtroom when Dr. Campbell laid bare for all present her poor ravaged body, showing every sign of delivery from stretch marks to engorged breasts stony with backed up milk. If she was, it's impossible to imagine a more excruciating moment for her. But even if she had somehow blissfully removed herself, the details would be spelled out in the *Gazette* and the *Daily Witness* the next day, not just for the consumption of those who had attended the trial, but for everyone in the city – and outside – who cared to read it.

The testimony of the last three witnesses of the afternoon could only be an anti climax after Dr. Campbell's performance, even though the next one, Dr. Gilbert Girdwood, was one of Canada's leading nineteenth-century scientists. An English-born physician and surgeon with a passion for chemistry, over the course of a long career Dr. Girdwood became an expert in forensic medicine and a noted medical-legal consultant.

Among his many talents and interests, Dr. Girdwood listed photography. In the winter of 1864-1865, newly arrived in Montreal from England, where recent experiments had demonstrated the utility of the magnesium flare as a light source, he taught William Notman the knack of creating firelight to illuminate nighttime pictures, a technique Notman used to great effect.

Dr. Girdwood was called to the stand on account of his expertise in chemical analysis. He stated that on March 26 High Constable Bissonette had given him the bottle of medicine found in Margaret's trunk. Girdwood examined the contents under microscope and now gave a nuanced report about what he had found. "From my examination I am of the opinion that the bottle had contained ergot of rye. Ergot is a diseased condition of rye, and all grasses are subject to a similar disease; ergot of wheat under the microscope, also of barley, and of common grasses present almost the same appearance, and produce almost the same effect. I have known it used to promote uterine action, which occasions the expulsion of anything obstructing the uterus. I believe it is commonly used to produce miscarriage. Some people doubt its efficacy but it is generally [so] used."

Under cross-examination by Kerr, Girdwood demonstrated his up-to-date grasp of the medical literature. He explained that ergot of rye was frequently used in medicine and was not necessarily always noxious. According to his measured response, "it is noxious or otherwise, according to the circumstances in which it is used, and the quantity administered."

The last two witnesses were Letitia Chambers and Ann Seymour, wife of John Barry. Miss Chambers testified that she had been housekeeper at the St. Lawrence Hall for four months. When they checked in on February 22 she was under the impression that the couple in rooms 103 and 104 were married. On Monday one of the chambermaids informed her that the lady in the room was very ill. She herself did not visit the room until Tuesday, when she determined that, indeed, this was the case. By Thursday morning, Miss Galbraith's condition had clearly greatly worsened. On that day, Notman asked her if she had heard about Dr. Patton's death. "I had seen Dr. Patton going in and out of the room; when he was not in, prisoner was there; Miss Galbraith did not seem to be ever left alone." Here was another example of Robert's continuing sense of responsibility for Margaret's welfare.

Ann Seymour next testified that she had been a chambermaid at the Hall for the past five years. In the only significant part of her testimony, which corroborated the chronology already established, she stated that on Sunday morning, "I was called in to empty the slops, and I saw blood therein."

It was 5:30 in the afternoon when the court adjourned. It had been a very long day.

CHAPTER THIRTEEN

Mr. Murray, Mr. Wilson, and Mr. Hogan Have Their Say

BY TEN O'CLOCK Tuesday morning April 21, hundreds of people were being turned away from the portals of the *Palais de justice*. The juicy newspaper coverage of the previous day's proceedings had only increased the city's appetite for a free show. It had also raised an issue that remains pertinent a century and a half later: where to draw the line in the reportage of disturbing and controversial information. The sternly evangelical Christian *Daily Witness* in particular found itself chastised by its readers. "We have received several letters condemning our course in publishing the evidence in the Notman trial, – all of them taking the ground that the *Witness*, as a religious paper, is admitted into families, and therefore ought not to insert anything that is unsuitable for ladies and young persons." Editor John Dougall explained that, after a great deal of soul-searching, he had concluded that while it was true that the *Witness* was a religious paper, it could not forget its general mandate as a newspaper "and the public have a right to expect the news in it, more especially if it be anything of peculiar interest and notoriety in the city." Though Dougall had deliberately suppressed some of the most flagrant details, he believed that his coverage remained balanced, and strengthened the cause of morality. "When Providence brings out a tremendous lesson of the shame, agony, and suffering connected with breaches of the divine law, why should the facts be hid? They constitute the most powerful sermon in favour of morality that could be preached or published."

Among those eager to learn lessons in either morality, human frailty, or birth control were many young people who, as on the previous day, "were rigidly excluded." The sharp-eyed reporter for the *Morning Chronicle* noted that on this second day of the trial, Robert Notman appeared "slightly restless and paler than yesterday but still puts on a good face." The expectation, however, was that this would be the day the prosecution would bring the prisoner to bay.

But once the judge took his seat, it also became clear that the defence had something up its sleeve. As the first witness was being sworn in, Bernard Devlin inquired whether Miss Galbraith was in attendance. Though the prosecution had finished with her the previous day, Ramsay responded in the affirmative.

The first witness of the day was F.W.L. Penton, Chief of Police, whom we encountered at Dr. Patton's inquest. Chief Penton said he had arrested Robert Notman on March 3, based on information he had received in connection with the death of Dr. Patton. This information had come to him through the agency of one "Mr. Murray." Based on what he had learned, Penton had searched Margaret Galbraith's lodgings and found letters from Notman, along with certain bottles of medicine. Confronted with these items, Notman "admitted his improper intimacy with Miss Galbraith," but denied the abortion-related charges.

Robert Murray was called to the stand. He would prove a most convincing witness, his testimony corroborated by Walter Wilson, Margaret Galbraith's landlord, who testified after him. Taken together, the story the two men recounted fleshed out the case that the prosecution had been so assiduously assembling.

On the morning of February 27 – a day after Dr. Patton's untimely death and a day before news of it was splashed across the newspapers – Murray and Wilson ran into each other on busy McGill Street in the heart of the city's business district. Wilson, a plumber and pipefitter, had come in search of Murray. Murray's wholesale business in petroleum, benzene, and lubricating oils was housed at 36 Lemoine, off McGill, and he had been out running an errand when Wilson buttonholed him. Wilson was deeply perturbed about the whereabouts of Miss Galbraith. Breathless with worry and the cold, for it was a chilly morning, he told Murray that he had not seen the girl since Saturday afternoon when she had left his house, telling him and his wife that she was going to sit with Mrs. Notman Senior, who – she said – was ill.

Mr. Murray had been instrumental in Miss Galbraith moving in with the Wilsons. A friend of the Galbraiths, like them he was from

Dumbartonshire in Scotland, and knew Margaret and her family ever since she came to Canada three years earlier. Murray lived in a genteel and upscale boarding house run by a Mrs. J. McArthur on Lagauchetiere Street, a short distance from the Wilsons. The Wilsons did not normally take in boarders, but were sympathetic to Mr. Murray's protégée, who was unhappy at her former lodgings with Mrs. Tannock.

Stamping his feet and rubbing his mittened hands together, Mr. Wilson peppered Mr. Murray with the reasons for his concern. The previous evening, using the pretext of a letter that had arrived for Miss Galbraith from her brother, he and Mrs. Wilson had called on Mrs. Notman in search of the girl. They did not find her there. Nor, according to an icy Mrs. Notman, had she been there at all.

Murray did not treat Wilson's concerns lightly. He said he knew where he could obtain the services of a detective, and asked Wilson if he had time to accompany him to make these arrangements. Then, after dispatching the investigator to make his inquiries, Murray and Wilson hastened to Mrs. Tannock's, where again they reached a dead end. By noon, Wilson had mentioned to Murray that Miss Galbraith had a trunk in her bedroom at his house. When they met up next with the detective, the latter suggested that it was a strong likelihood that Mr. Robert Notman was implicated in the case. At the mention of Miss Galbraith's trunk, he urged searching it for the possibility of letters. They discovered that its hinges had been broken off. (This mystery was never solved, but more than likely the detective's hand had been at work.)

Murray, squeamish at the idea of violating Miss Galbraith's privacy, said they must first speak with Chief Penton. According to Walter Wilson's testimony, Penton advised them to take a look at the letters.

Robert Murray cared about Margaret, whether romantically or as a friend is unknown. Having located the trunk with its cache of correspondence in her room, he examined only two letters. Their contents enraged him. He saw no need to read further. Grim faced, he told the other two men that they must head for Notman's office on Peter Street.

When they arrived, the detective stayed outside in the bitter February afternoon. Robert Murray seethed at the sight of Notman blinking at his unannounced visitors and half rising from behind his desk in the inner office.

"Where is Miss Galbraith?"

"I don't know," Notman dithered. "Why do you ask me that question?"

"You do know, I know that you know, and unless you tell me where she is, I will telegraph for her father or her brother!"

"I do not know where she is, but if you'll allow me till five o'clock I think I can find out where she is."

Walter Wilson piped up that it was no use denying the obvious, they had come with knowledge of Notman's intimate affairs written in his own hand. Wilson added, "We have spent the forenoon over this matter and couldn't do better than go with you and help you find her." At this point, Notman showed Wilson the door. Afterwards Wilson concluded that Notman asked him to leave the room because he had spoken so sharply. But given what Notman said to Murray after Wilson withdrew to the outer office, it's as likely that Notman felt more comfortable confiding in someone of his own class and age, rather than a crusty old tradesman.

Once they were on their own, Notman seemed almost eager to confess. He told Murray that he had had "connection" with Miss Galbraith some five months earlier and "unfortunately … got her with child." Despite making every effort in his power "to stop it," he had been completely unsuccessful until the Saturday night that he arranged for the two of them to go to the St. Lawrence Hall "for the purpose of being relieved." Notman assured Murray that he had "made her as comfortable as possible by hiring two rooms for her." The operation had worked and, according to Notman, the patient was now doing as well as could be expected. Alas, however, the doctor who attended her had been found dead. He invited Murray to accompany him to the Hall, to see how very comfortable her accommodations were. On the way, they would also look for another doctor to replace poor Dr. Patton. He wanted only the finest to be had, expressing a preference for either Craik or Campbell.

Murray recalled that he had difficulty maintaining his composure when he asked Notman if "Saturday night [was] the first operation?" Notman nodded assent. Murray then quoted from memory

Notman's own words in a letter to Margaret: "'I would rather that affair had not been done. However, I hope it has given the desired effect....'" What exactly had he meant by that?

"Oh that was a simple sponge affair," came the reply.

Accompanying Notman to the St. Lawrence Hall, Murray entered the suite and found Margaret in bed in Room 104. He was further shaken at her pallor and the fact that she was so weak she was unable to hold a teacup to her lips. This was before Dr. Campbell's visit, before a nurse had been ordered. Putting aside his revulsion for Notman in the higher cause of trying to save the girl, Murray suggested that Mrs. Wilson come by the following morning.

True to his word, Murray escorted Mrs. Wilson to the hotel on Friday, but out of delicacy did not intrude upon the sick room a second time. Instead, he visited Notman at his office that afternoon to inquire after Margaret's health. During this particular interview Notman babbled on in a stream of consciousness monologue that Margaret "was a most extraordinary girl." He had, he said, "given her enough of medicine to operate upon a dozen girls." He had administered the doses in his own office, where she used "to come... in the evening, ... and take her medicine." In the witness box, Murray recalled that Notman said that sometimes Dr. Patton was present, and sometimes not. Before his arrest, Notman also dropped by Murray's office a couple of times to report on Margaret's health.

After Notman was taken into custody, Murray visited him at the police station. Whether this was out of the goodness of his heart or, more likely, in order to assist the police is uncertain. Under cross-examination by Devlin, Murray admitted that policemen were present in the police office while he was talking with Notman, and may have overheard a snatch of critical conversation between them. Notman had asked him if he had taken the letters in the trunk away with him. Murray's emphatic "*No*" was printed in italics by the papers.

"My God!" Notman exclaimed. "There is enough there to send me to the Penitentiary." He asked Murray as a favour to use the word "miscarriage" – instead of "abortion" – if the case came to trial by jury.

The cross-examination that followed Robert Murray's testimony was savagely adversarial. Bernard Devlin was on the warpath, his strategy being to further discredit Margaret Galbraith, and imply that not only was she Robert Notman's mistress, but Robert Murray's as well.

Murray would have none of it. Brilliant and belligerent as Devlin was, he had met his match in an intelligent and unintimidated witness.

In response to Devlin's insinuating queries, Murray responded that he had been introduced to Miss Galbraith by his brother, who lived on St. Elisabeth Street (that would have been bookkeeper John Murray) and that he knew her "intimately." (Again, as with Mr. Benning and Dr. Patton, this implied friendship, not erotic love.) Although he once accompanied her to the Rivière-des-Prairies – the Back River – on a sleighing party that set out from the Wilsons', he was not in the habit of calling upon her in the evenings. The party had consisted of a large group, some twenty or thirty people.

No, he was not related to Miss Galbraith and no, he was not married. No, he did not break open her trunk to get at the letters. Yes, he had repeatedly visited her in hospital at the request of her father. He had gained admission to the hospital on a pass from Mr. McLennan, even though he – Murray – wasn't a relative.

The motivation for businessman Hugh McLennan's involvement in the affairs of Margaret Galbraith was more than likely Scottish clannishness. Born in Glengarry County, Upper Canada, in 1825 to a Scottish immigrant father, McLennan moved to Montreal as a teenager and made a fortune in shipping and grain. A longtime supporter of the Montreal Art Association and of the St. Andrew's Society (like William Notman), he clearly had pull at the General Hospital. Possibly at the request of Archibald Galbraith, he had interceded on behalf of an unfortunate Scottish girl. Mr. McLennan was not a policeman, continued Robert Murray in cross-examination by Devlin; perhaps he was a magistrate. No one – Murray had to reiterate this several times – no one besides Miss Galbraith's father and Mr. McLennan, certainly not Mr. Ramsay, ever asked him to speak or give advice to her about the trial.

How often had he visited her? He couldn't say precisely – perhaps five, or six, or even more times! On almost all those occasions, her father was there as well. Maybe on a couple of occasions he and she were alone. Those conversations each lasted perhaps half an hour.

Devlin pressed the point: had Murray been told to give Miss Galbraith advice about how she should testify? Did they speak of the trial together?

Yes, Murray said. "I spoke to her about the trial. [But] I did not tell her that if she did not give evidence... she would be held responsible herself. I told her to speak the truth.... I never asked her the particulars of the case.... All that we spoke about was simply the facts which had appeared in the newspapers."

A rapid-fire exchange between counsel and witness ensued.

Devlin: "What appeared in the newspapers?"

Murray: "You know yourself."

Devlin: "How do you know that I read the newspapers?"

Murray: "I have seen you read them."

Unable to rattle the witness, Devlin changed tactics and asked him why he found it necessary to visit Margaret in the first place.

"The girl was almost alone here, and I know her almost from the time she came from the same place in Scotland as myself. She is an intelligent girl, and quite able to speak on other subjects beside the trial. I went up to speak to her as any friend of her father's... would do, nothing more."

A smug *Gazette* reported that Devlin's cross-examination did not benefit Robert Notman, Murray remaining "remarkably cool, and proving himself much more than a match for the astute counsel."

The last witness for the prosecution was Henry Hogan, proprietor and manager of the St. Lawrence Hall. Hogan at this time was forty-eight years old, affable of manner and shrewd in his judgments. He had seen and heard much since opening for business in 1851, and knew when to speak and when to remain silent. In the decade leading up to the Notman trial, his establishment had been temporary home to a host of celebrities. When the Prince of Wales came to open the Victoria Bridge in the summer of 1860, his aristocratic retinue was put up at the Hall and had no complaints about the level of attentive service and sumptuous banquet tables. Among high society guests, Henry Hogan also entertained governors general and Sir William Fenwick (a hero of the Crimean War and possible bastard half-brother to Queen Victoria), who was Commander-in-Chief of forces in British North America.

British forces were much in evidence at the Hall after the international crisis sparked by the raiding of HMS *Trent* by the United States Navy in the fall of 1861. On that notorious occasion, two diplomatic agents of the Confederate States were seized by American seamen on the British ship. Britain was outraged at this violation of her sovereignty on the seas, and appeared poised to enter the American Civil War as an ally of the Confederacy. Should this have been the case, Montreal – so close to the border with the North – would have become a plum target for Northern troops.

So many British soldiers now streamed into the city that the overflow was housed at the St. Lawrence Hall, which became the de facto headquarters of the local British garrison. The war correspondent of the London *Times* was staying at the Hall and described its corridors as filled with an "abundance of soldiers, anxious orderlies with quaint quartoes full of orders, and military idlers smoking as much as you like, but, I am glad to say, not chewing...." Beneath twinkling crystal chandeliers that flashed in the gaslight of the dining room, officers' red uniforms contrasted with the sheen of the damask tablecloths and serviettes. Volleys of tipsy laughter mingled with the clatter of fancy china, while faint echoes of sleigh bells on St. James Street drifted in through the double windows.

The *Trent* imbroglio was settled through diplomatic channels, but Britain – and much of Montreal – continued to sympathize with the Southern States. Confederate guests were treated royally at the Hall, and this generous reception coupled with the city's proximity to the border made the hotel an attractive haven for Confederate spies. In the mid-1860s, Jacob Thompson, one of the chief plotters of the assassination of President Lincoln, spent lengthy sojourns there and boasted of plans to rid the world "of the tyrant Lincoln."

Late in life, Henry Hogan liked to share memories of the most infamous of the Hall's guests. Hogan had been much taken by John Wilkes Booth, whose looks and acting talent he greatly admired. Booth spent time in Montreal in 1864 and 1865, ostensibly trying to work at the Theatre Royal on Coté Street, but mostly hatching schemes against the president. Hogan remininisced that Booth "was here just a week or ten days before the assassination of Lincoln. In fact when the news reached here it was recalled by the friends of Booth that just before leaving Montreal he told them they would hear in a very short time of something that would startle the world." Hogan believed that, if not for the crazed deed for which he would pay with his life, Booth "might have become one of the greatest actors of his epoch."

But there was a great difference for the hotelier between hosting a celebrity villain and hosting a tarnished young woman, her lover, and her abortionist. He made it very clear in his testimony for the Crown that the Hall did not need notoriety of the sort invited by Robert Notman's custom.

"I am owner of the St. Lawrence Hall," stated Mr. Hogan in the witness box. "On the 28th of February, I was told by my clerk that prisoner had engaged rooms 103 and 104 for a Miss Williams from South Stukely." On hearing from his chambermaid that the lady in question appeared to be sick, Hogan asked to see Mr. Notman. "I told him it was rather strange that he should have a lady friend in those rooms and no one had access to them except himself and the doctor. He replied there was nothing wrong; the lady would be well in a day or two and would go." This explanation did not cut it with Henry Hogan. "I said, Mr. Notman, are you aware that when a lady is sick, it is for the chambermaid or housekeeper to visit her and not a gentleman?' He repeated that nothing was wrong, and I replied, 'I have my doubts.'"

A couple of days later, after he had had a chat with Mrs. Wilson who had been visiting Miss Galbraith, Hogan once more sent for Notman. "I told him that from the first moment I was convinced it was all wrong... and I said to him, 'Mr. Notman, had not the lady been sick, I would put both you and her out of the house: you might have found many other places for your object besides my house.'" According to Hogan, Notman apologized and said that the lady would be leaving soon.

CHAPTER FOURTEEN

The Defence Fights Back

COUNSEL FOR THE DEFENCE returned to the courtroom after the noon break, determined to fight by any and all means. After taking issue with the wording of the indictment and being soundly rebuffed by Judge Drummond – let the defence stop stalling and hairsplitting and present their case – William Kerr called his first witness: "Miss Margaret Galbraith!"

There was a sharp collective intake of breath in the chamber. Miss Galbraith had been the prosecution's hot property the day before. How came she now to be testifying for the other side?

What array of thoughts and emotions shot through Margaret as she clambered to her feet? When she entered the courthouse that morning as a spectator, had she spotted a face in the lobby and then quickly averted her own, as her heart began to hammer? Had she placed herself on full alert, quivering with an animal instinct for self-preservation? If so, it did not show now. As she approached the witness stand, she succumbed to none of hysterics of the day before. She took the stand alone, with no Letitia Chambers by her side, armed only with her own wits.

Under questioning by Kerr she corroborated Robert Murray's testimony of the morning. She had known Mr. Murray for about three years. He had called on her frequently in hospital, on average three times a week. She was precise about the length of her hospital stay: she had been admitted on March 14, a Saturday, and discharged five weeks later, only two days prior to the commencement of the trial. Asked about Murray's advice to her, she responded, "I was told to tell the truth, and the whole truth, whatever might be the consequences either to myself or the prisoner."

And now came the question she had hoped no one would ever ask.

Did she know Dr. MacCallum?

Quite possibly she had not shared the answer to this question with either Robert Notman or Robert Murray. Certainly not with prosecutor Ramsay.

"I do not know Dr. MacCallum."

A stocky, pleasant-looking man with an open countenance and air of authority stepped forward.

Did she recognize him?

No, she did not.

Had she ever consulted him?

Never. She had never called on Dr. MacCallum with reference to her illness, nor sought advice from any doctor save Dr. Patton.

The Crown waived its right to cross-examine. Scenting danger to his elaborately structured case, Ramsay was thinking fast.

At forty-four years of age, Dr. Duncan Campbell MacCallum was at the height of his powers and of his career. A McGill medical graduate who had also studied in London, Edinburgh, and Dublin, he was Montreal's pre-eminent English-speaking gynecologist and obstetrician, in charge of the University Lying-In Hospital and Professor of Midwifery and Diseases of Women and Children at McGill.

Dr. MacCallum took the oath, and upon being asked whether he knew Robert Notman replied, "I know the prisoner by sight, and I have spoken to him. I also know his brother by eyesight."

And what about the last witness?

"I have once seen the last witness, Miss Galbraith."

Ramsay leapt to his feet with two objections. This line of questioning was intended to impugn Miss Galbraith's credibility. It was entirely irrelevant to the case. Furthermore, Miss Galbraith was the defence's own witness. Her testimony could not be attacked by them.

Kerr made an impassioned – the *Gazette* called it a "very violent" – speech, asking for "even handed justice." He had this morning received a note in court asking whether "the fact of this girl, Miss Galbraith, having consulted another doctor, in order to procure abortion, be of any avail in this case?" He, Mr. Kerr, then stepped out of the courtroom and found Dr. MacCallum, the present witness, in the lobby, ready to swear to such evidence.

Judge Drummond ruled that the defence had no right to cast doubt on the evidence of their own witness.

Kerr shouted over him. He had important new evidence at hand! "[Am I] to be shut out?"

Ramsay yelled back, "You are!"

Kerr addressed the jury about of the crucial nature of this new evidence, decrying the way justice was being carried out in this courtroom. Judge Drummond raised his voice as he ruled Dr. MacCallum's evidence inadmissible.

In that case, said Kerr, still evidently agitated, the defence would assail Miss Galbraith's credibility in her evidence for the Crown the previous day.

Judge Drummond refused to permit this. If the defence had selected Miss Galbraith as a witness, they must have had faith in her. He upheld the prosecution's objections.

Kerr had no choice but to curb his temper and try a new tack. He put another question to Dr. MacCallum. "Did Margaret Galbraith call on you eight or nine weeks before Notman's arrest, and request you to give her medicines to procure an abortion?"

Ramsay again objected. The question was irrelevant.

Again Judge Drummond upheld the objection.

Kerr asked Dr. MacCallum if he had mentioned these facts for the first time only this morning.

Ramsay objected on the grounds that there were no "facts."

Judge Drummond maintained the objection.

With that, the defence was done presenting its witnesses. To some, the evidence tasted like thin broth. To others, it admitted a chink of hope for Robert Notman.

Both Kerr and Devlin proceeded to speak at length on behalf of the prisoner. First, Kerr addressed the jury for half an hour in what the *Gazette* called "a highly ingenious effort." He reminded them that it had been exceedingly difficult to put together an unprejudiced jury because popular sentiment ran so high against the defendant. He then boldly needled the judge, saying it was as much his duty as that of the jury to remain open-minded.

In outlining the facts of the case, Kerr focused on the fact that Notman was in Toronto when Miss Galbraith had sought out Dr. Patton. At that time, Margaret Galbraith was not sure she was pregnant.

Once Dr. Patton ascertained this, it was she who petitioned him for an abortion, not the prisoner. Kerr added that the expression of regret by the prisoner in a letter from Toronto referred to a procedure made at Miss Galbraith's own request.

He reminded the jury of Dr. Girdwood's statement that ergot of rye was not necessarily a noxious thing. Alluding to Robert Murray and Walter Wilson, Kerr accused the prosecution of having been conducted by "friends of Miss Galbraith." He placed the blame for the abortion squarely on the girl, who "finding that the name and fame of herself and family were at stake, implored the prisoner to obtain for her all the medical treatment which was afterwards bestowed upon her. Brought up as she had been, it must have been her most earnest desire to get rid of the burden which her imprudence had brought upon her."

Kerr went on to say that when the defence had tried to show Miss Galbraith's determination and intention to obtain an abortion, they were told that it was too late for Dr. MacCallum to speak. In fact, whenever evidence favourable to the prisoner was introduced, technical objections thwarted its presentation.

In his summing-up speech, Bernard Devlin fully lived up to his reputation as a showman trial lawyer. For a full hour and twenty-five minutes, he alternately pleaded with and harangued the jury. Honey-tongued and passionate, he cajoled, flattered, and nitpicked by turn. Even the *Gazette's* reporter, whose sympathies lay entirely with the prosecution, succumbed to his combination of charm, flattery, and legal adroitness, and called his address eloquent and able.

Devlin opened by saying that it was not his purpose to shield a guilty man, but to petition for a fair and honest trial for an innocent one. The jurymen must discard their biases. A crime such as the one the prisoner was accused of ought to be punished, but in a case where the evidence was inconclusive, their duty was to acquit.

Point by point, he poked holes in the prosecution's case, maintaining that it was based purely on Miss Galbraith's account of events. She had said that she had obtained a bottle of medicine from Dr. Patton. The Crown had produced a bottle that Dr. Girdwood said contained ergot of rye. But the substance in it was so infinitesimally small, there had barely been enough to examine under a microscope. This special bottle was then left uncorked in a trunk. After the passage of several weeks, Miss Galbraith could only say the dregs looked to be the same in colour as what she recalled. She did not claim that the contents were what Dr. Patton had placed in it.

Devlin said he knew in advance what Mr. Ramsay would say to this argument: they had not only the girl's evidence, but also the testimony of an eminent scientist in the person of Dr. Girdwood. But there were all sorts of possibilities to account for the presence of the ergot of rye in the bottle. How could it be proved that Dr. Patton had placed that particular substance into the vial? Might it not have contained remains of that substance prior to the prescription Dr. Patton placed in it? A "man's life, character, honour, must not be swept away by doubts." However strongly the jury suspected that the bottle had contained ergot of rye, they must give the benefit of the doubt to the prisoner.

Devlin next spoke of the prisoner's loose connection with the actual administration of the purported noxious substance. The fact that Miss Galbraith met Dr. Patton at Mr. Notman's office did not in any way imply or prove that she went there to obtain an abortion. She had testified that she did not know what was wrong with her when she consulted the doctor. In that case, how could the prisoner have known? And where was the prisoner when the doctor gave her the medicine? Three hundred miles away in Toronto! How could it then be said that he counselled, procured, and commanded Dr. Patton to administer to her a certain noxious drug, called ergot of rye? There was "not one tittle of evidence" to prove that before the 15th of December the prisoner had ever spoken a word to Dr. Patton about ergot of rye.

In fact, the latter portion of the evidence of Miss Galbraith showed that the medical treatment she subsequently received from Dr. Patton was at her own request. In the prisoner's letter of December 18, dated from Toronto, he said, "I feel very bad, as I would rather that affair had not been done." These words referred to the examination of Miss Galbraith and the medicine which had been given her by Dr. Patton and had nothing to do with the prisoner's own actions.

In conclusion, Devlin urged the Crown to admit that there was no case to put before a jury. He appealled to the jury to disregard public prejudice against the prisoner and bravely deliver an unpopular verdict.

The last words of the afternoon of the second day came from prosecutor T. K. Ramsay. Summing up for the Crown, predictably he slashed out at the defence. "A great many people thought that every prosecution was a persecution," he began, and said he hoped the jury was not so credulous as to be swayed by counsel's insinuation that the full force of the state was being used to convict an innocent man. In a voice laced with sarcasm, Ramsay apologized if he was tiring the jury by presenting them with hard facts. Indeed they must be tired, "after the defence had gone on for two hours without calling a single witness" and had succeeded only in "trying to talk common sense out of the jurors' heads.... All this bombast, all these long speeches only contained a very... bad argument." In turn, he rehashed the prosecution's case, firstly underlining Dr. Patton's guilt, an example of which was the lack of a label on the bottle of ergot of rye, the noxious substance vouched for by Dr. Girdwood. Concerning Dr. Patton, "what inference should be drawn from the conduct of a doctor who gave a medicine whose name he carefully erased?"

Like Devlin, Ramsay was a master of the colourful and memorable phrase. Having to his own satisfaction proven the guilt of the physician, he moved on to the complicity of the prisoner. The case, he said, could only have been clearer if "the criminal went and rang a bell... and asked the public to witness his actions." Alluding to Robert Murray's testimony, Ramsay reminded the jury that Notman had confessed to having administered drugs to Miss Galbraith. As to Margaret being a willing party, "Undoubtedly she was, but that did not alter the guilt of the prisoner." He – Ramsay – did not want to bear the responsibility of such a guilty party escaping justice.

The defence had "danced ... Dr. MacCallum before the jury's eyes," and raised "a great row ... because his evidence was refused. This had nothing to do with the case. The evidence was excluded because it was illegal and irrelevant...." Their purpose was not to try an "unfortunate girl who had striven to hide her shame." Nor could they compare any question of her guilt to that of the prisoner.

He requested that the jury remember the full text of Notman's letter of December 18 that the defence had emphasized to great effect.

The words, in full, were, *"I would rather that affair had not been done, – however, I hope it has given the desired effect, and you will go home lighter in body and mind."* Neither should they forget Notman's exclamation, at the police station, regarding another letter, "My God! There is enough in that letter to send me to the penitentiary."

Concluding an hour-long speech that the *Gazette* found powerfully damaging to the prisoner, Ramsay called attention to the prominence of the Notman family. "The jury must not let themselves be swayed by appeals to sympathy, because prisoner's brother has a respectable position in society, and because jury might have seen him walking along the street."

CHAPTER FIFTEEN

"Breathless Silence"

FIRST THING WEDNESDAY morning, Judge Drummond requested that Miss Galbraith return to the witness box. He asked her to answer two questions of utmost gravity: when had she become aware of her pregnancy, and had she ever felt the baby move? These points cut directly to the heart of the prisoner's situation: procuring abortion after quickening was a felony punishable by death for the person performing an abortion. In this case the abortionist being dead, Notman as his accomplice stood to take the rap.

"I first perceived that I was in a state of pregnancy about the end of October."

With this response Margaret put aside all pretense of being ignorant of her condition when she first consulted Dr. Patton in December. (How, indeed, could she – the oldest of ten children, bearing witness to her mother's serial pregnancies virtually all her life – have been oblivious to her own symptoms?)

"I am not aware that I perceived any motion of the child." This was probably true, as in a first pregnancy it is difficult to detect the initial airy flutterings of the foetus. If, on the other hand, she had felt the baby move, she was perjuring herself in order to protect Robert.

The chamber was "considerably crowded" in anticipation of the judge's summing-up and charge to the jury. If there had been any doubt over the course of the past two days as to Drummond's leanings, they were about to be dispelled. For His Honour, this was not just the case of the Queen versus Robert Notman, it was about "nipping in the bud ... one of the greatest curses that could afflict a country," the nation to the south being the first one to spring to mind. Was Canada to emulate "the vicious example of other lands, in which, where a hundred years ago, families were numbered by tens or twelves, now [they] only counted one and two? The cause was abortion."

In a speech lasting eighty minutes and drawing on English, French, and Canadian precedents, Drummond made mincemeat of the defence's arguments and aligned himself squarely with Ramsay, who, he said, had presented his case so ably as to make his own task simple. The judge prefaced his remarks with the statement that abortion held within it the potential for double murder. "The jury would judge if the prisoner would be allowed to sacrifice not only the life of his unborn illegitimate child, but also risk the chance of killing the woman who had given her Honour for her guilty love for him. Are such things to be allowed?"

Dr. Girdwood, His Honour said, had ably pointed out that ergot of rye could sometimes be used for legitimate medical purposes. Drummond then performed a little fancy footwork: "If applied to assist a woman in difficult legitimate labour, it was innoxious. But when administered to a young, to an unmarried woman, avowedly to procure an abortion, it was noxious." Nor need it be proved that a woman was pregnant, "the intention is all that is wanted. When medicine is administered with intent to produce an abortion it became a crime."

He dismissed out of hand "the unheard of doctrine" that the prisoner had to be physically present to be complicit with Dr. Patton. Were they not living in the age of the telegraph? With such revolutionary means of communications, "one might be accessory to a crime committed in California or Australia."

In this case, the prisoner was corresponding with Miss Galbraith and egging her on. Drummond read Robert's letters out loud, underlining their compromising nature, in particular the one in which he expressed regret and to which the defence had foolishly called attention. He continued by recounting Robert Murray's and Margaret Galbraith's testimonies in detail. Drummond praised Murray for his clear and dispassionate delivery and "unusual happiness of memory." Taking another jab at the defence, he reminded the jury of the graceful manner that Murray had emerged from a scathing cross-examination "in which every effort was made to cast insinuations on his acquaintance with Miss Galbraith and his object in visiting her." Mr. Murray's behaviour had been exemplary. His visits to Miss Galbraith in hospital were gestures of compassion taken at her father's behest "because she was a friendless invalid amongst strangers, in a strange land."

In bringing his charge to conclusion, the judge was clearly still smarting from the accusations of partiality levelled at him by Kerr the day before. "The defence had attempted in a very impressive tone to strike terror into the heart of the judge, and the manner in which he was warned of the consequences resulting from his action was something terrible." He would not be swayed by such denunciations. "I must tell you very distinctly that the judge has a right to express his opinion, and that the jury have a right to demand his assistance, based on long experience, not only as to the law, but even as to the facts of the case." They were not bound to follow his opinion, but it behooved them to hear out his interpretation of the law.

"When we consider how difficult it is to prove such a case which frequently rests on circumstantial evidence, it appears to me marvelous how such an accumulation of proof could have been gathered against the unfortunate prisoner. It leaves no reasonable doubt in the mind of any reasonable man." He had never "seen, heard, or read" of a case as ironclad as this one.

With these instructions, the jury withdrew at eleven thirty.

While they were deliberating, the judge began hearing a capital case against one George Wilson, a soldier who had killed his captain while toxically drunk. The trial had hardly begun when recess was called, and immediately upon the resumption of proceedings at one o'clock, Judge Drummond – his mind clearly more occupied with the Notman case than the one before him – sent word to the jury inquiring about their progress. A message came back that they were not in agreement, and had no idea when they would be.

According to the *Gazette*, the courtroom was filled "to suffocation." No one – including the hapless George Wilson – appeared to have much interest in anything but the Notman verdict. "The reporters were idle, and the audience *nonchalant*. The nature of the crime and the social position of the prisoner made … [it] the lion of the day." Finally, after an interval of nearly four hours, the jury returned, and on being asked by the judge if they had agreed on a verdict, their foreman replied: "We find the prisoner guilty of participating in the act, but not of administering the medicine in person."

Jubilant, Devlin exclaimed that this was a verdict of not guilty. There was a terse exchange between him and the judge, who appeared near the end of his tether with frustration. "I must request, Mr. Devlin, that you do not interrupt me at the very moment when I have a solemn duty to perform."

Devlin snapped back: "So do I."

Ignoring him, Drummond turned towards the foreman. "He is not charged with administering the medicine," he explained in exasperation, "but with counseling, procuring, and commanding *Dr. Patton* to administer it." He instructed them to reread the indictment: in it Dr. Patton was charged with administering the medicine, and the prisoner with having induced him to do so. They must return a verdict of either guilty or not guilty, nothing more or less.

The jury once more departed, leaving behind them – in the words of the *Gazette* – "intense excitement" and a "deadly pale" prisoner.

An hour and a half later, as testimony in the George Wilson case dragged on, an officer of the court approached Drummond and whispered in his ear. The jury stood clumped at the threshold of the chamber; it was now a few minutes before five. Judge Drummond beckoned them to enter. In they shambled, a dozen men, their body language – rounded shoulders, evasive eyes, bemused expressions – sheepish. The judge regarded them sternly. He had heard, he said, "that they desired some information. What was it?"

One Guillaume Chouinard stepped forward. He had some scruples, he said, about the indictment. "The prisoner was charged with administering poison –"

"The prisoner was not charged with anything of the sort," shouted His Honour. Chouinard replied that he had seen it in the paper with his own eyes.

"What paper?"

"The *Herald*."

Out tumbled the story, and it caused His Honour no small embarrassment. It had been he who had read out loud Robert Notman's letters in court from a version printed in the *Herald*, as they were easier to decipher than the handwritten originals. But – he scolded – the jurors had no business consulting newspapers! Well, if the Deputy Clerk of the Crown had – perhaps inadvertently – allowed them to see the paper, it was solely for the purpose of reading the letters.

The wretched jurors tried to explain that they had read a version of the indictment printed in the same copy of the *Herald* as the letters. Well, they had no business taking their instructions from newspapers! He would once more go over the correct version of the indictment. They were to come back only if they had made up their minds whether the prisoner was guilty or not guilty.

It was past five o'clock when the browbeaten jury withdrew for the third time. The court normally adjourned at 5:30.

The defence lawyers were on their feet, protesting and expostulating. The jury had been given a garbled and biased report. Mr. Devlin could remember the case of "the mulatoo [*sic*], Leo, who was undergoing his trial for rape. The jury was being sent from court for the night, when one of them slipped away from the rest, to put up his shutters. A verdict of guilty was returned, but prisoner was discharged." He asked for the court to be adjourned until the next day so that he could look for other precedents.

The judge would have none of it. They must hear the verdict.

At 5:18 the jury returned for the third time. "Every preparation had been made to adjourn the court," wrote the *Gazette*, "the crier was in the box, the space within the bar was crowded with lawyers, and every one had left his seat. The jury averted their eyes from the prisoner who was very pale, the lines on his face showing more markedly than before.

"Amid breathless silence the names of the jurors were called…."

Patrick Curley,
William Hart,
James Delany,
William Crow,
Michael Delaney,
William Hannan,
Alfred Cooper,
Charles Higgins,
William Murphy,
Calixte Berthiaume,
Guillaume Chouinard,
X. H. Leclair.

Each in turn was asked the fateful question, "Do you find the prisoner guilty or not guilty as charged?"

Each in turn pronounced the word "guilty."

"The prisoner stood for a moment at the bar," wrote the *Gazette*, "and then stepping down seemed to stagger back into the dock.... Thus ended this *cause celebre* [*sic*], which was one of the most ably and successfully conducted on the part of the Crown that we have ever witnessed."

But the *Gazette* was wrong. The case had not ended. Arguably, it would not end until the lives of Robert Notman and Margaret Galbraith were over; perhaps not even with the death of their descendants. Even in the short term, it would not end until the sentence was pronounced.

As the hubbub in the courtroom gradually subsided, the audience trooping out onto the snowy streets in anticipation of animated dinner-table discussions, the defence spun into action. Devlin and Kerr had perhaps counted on their brilliance in the courtroom to dazzle judge and jury in the face of Ramsay's plodding performance. They may also have assumed a sympathetic hearing from Judge Drummond, who was known to be friendly with the Notman family. (At one point during the trial the judge claimed acquaintanceship with Robert since Robert's childhood – a clear impossibility, since Robert was already nineteen when he arrived in Montreal.) But they had been too cocky. Drummond had had the bit between his teeth from the start, and had proved completely unswayable, perhaps trying to lay to rest a guilty conscience from the days of the Patterson trial, when he had pleaded the case of the abortionist.

The irregular introduction of a newspaper into the sanctity of the jury room had handed them a golden opportunity. The two men used the next day to unearth exactly what had taken place in the jury room. It turned out that right after the jury withdrew for the third time, Clerk of the Crown Schiller had followed them into the jury room and informed them that if they did not come up with a verdict within the next five minutes, they would be locked up for a third night in a row because the court would adjourn at 5:30.

Two days later on Friday morning, April 24, Warren Hastings Kerr introduced three motions: first, that it should be entered into the record that a copy of the *Herald* of April 21 had been given to the jury; second, that the Notman trial should be declared a mistrial as a consequence and Notman be tried again; and last, that "the jury had been coerced and intimidated into rendering a verdict of guilty" by Schiller's threat.

Drummond's response was predictable. "This is insulting to the Court, sir. Intimidating the jury! I gave the order as information, requesting Mr. Schiller to ask the jury if they had agreed, adding that the Court would adjourn."

He also refused to enter the motions into the record, and stated that Canadian jurisprudence prevented him from granting a new trial in the case of a felony. The bickering went on for more than an hour, legal precedents being advanced by the defence from both British and American sources. At one point, prosecutor Ramsay snarled that perhaps "we would next introduce French law reports, and ultimately the Russian code." But the defence won a partial victory: while the judge completely exonerated Schiller from all censure, he said he would pronounce his opinions on the other two motions the following Monday.

This did not happen, because – as a small boxed announcement stated in the *Gazette* of Tuesday, April 28 – proceedings had to be postponed by a day, as the enervated judge had succumbed to a severe cold.

On Tuesday afternoon, with the court "crowded most uncomfortably – many prominent citizens taking an interest in the Notman case being present," the judge dismissed the defence's authorities and arguments, and quashed their motions. Drummond said that he had canvassed his fellow judges of the Queen's Bench, and they all agreed with him that under English law a new trial for this case could not be granted. The defence kept up a barrage of arguments for most of the afternoon, with the judge not ceding an inch. His final words on the subject were, "I admire the zeal of learned counsel for the defence; a lawyer should never neglect anything which may benefit his client, but I must declare the motions inadmissible."

The spectators, who had become restless during the course of the legal palaver, quietened at the announcement that His Honour was now to begin sentencing those who had been tried throughout the March term. While a few were being dispatched for relatively short stints to the Montreal Gaol, the bulk were destined for the Provincial Penitentiary in Kingston.

Finally those who were at the edge of their seats waiting to hear the fate of Robert Notman heard his name being called and saw him come forward to the front of the dock. Pale as chalk, he was dressed in black, his face impassive. He was asked if he had anything to say, but before he could open his mouth, Devlin was on his feet with a new set of objections, this time contesting the phrasing of the indictment, which he called contradictory. In the first count, Notman was charged with the administration "of a thing absolutely known to the Court, ergot of rye; in the last count he... [was] found guilty of administering a thing unknown to the jurors." He argued that if it was unknown to jurors, it couldn't be ergot of rye. This time he had stumped the judge. Feverish and befuddled by his cold, Drummond could not come up with a rejoinder. On top of it all, Ramsay was absent for the afternoon and the best that Ramsay's partner, L. S. Morin, could offer was that there had been no advance notice of the motion. His Honour metaphorically threw up his hands and adjourned the court until the following day, when Ramsay would be present.

A full week had elapsed since a guilty verdict had been extracted from the jury by the judge, and the wait for sentencing had stretched nerves to a breaking point. When His Honour took his seat on Wednesday, April 29 at noon, according to the *Gazette* of the next day "the Court was again densely crowded." The defence appeared to be clutching at new straws and stratagems. At the first opportunity, Kerr began attacking the manner in which the jury was originally struck, claiming it had been illegal. The judge ruled out this objection as coming too late.

Kerr melted down. "Are we to be refused the privilege of addressing the Court? We have been compelled to work against this sort of thing all through the trial."

"You have been compelled to work against a certain fixed knowledge of the law," the judge barked back, accusing the defence of employing "desperate arguments." Devlin entered the fray calling either for a writ of error or an arrest of judgement, and adding that the judge was "desirous" of passing hasty sentence.

It was Drummond's turn to melt down. "Desirous, Mr. Devlin! I, whose heart bleeds for the man whom I knew. It is the most painful duty I ever had to perform, such a painful duty that my health has almost broken down during the trial. In these last two days I have suffered more mental agony than in the rest of my life."

Devlin refused to give in. In a speech deemed eloquent and impressive by the press, he pleaded with the judge to defer passing sentence until a meeting of the Court of Appeals in June. If this came to pass, he – Devlin – would not be obliged to request a writ of error from the attorney general. He would accept any ruling – yea or nay – of the Court of Appeals. Justice would then have been served.

Drummond would brook no further interruptions. He declared that it was time to move on. If the indictment was contradictory, the defence had waited too long to raise the matter. "The material question was whether a noxious thing had been administered. There was no doubt of this. If I reserved my judgment I would be shrinking from the performance of a painful duty."

Drummond turned towards the prisoner to address him, and "breathless silence" settled over the room. "Robert Notman, I have said no truer words than those wrested from me a moment since, when your counsel charged me with a desire to inflict punishment upon you.... I know you, I had pleasure in knowing you, I esteemed and admired you amongst other things for the zealous and intelligent assistance you had rendered your brother in bringing to the highest possible perfection among us the most beautiful art of the age. I assure you it is one of the most painful acts of my life now to pass sentence on you."

Steeped in Victorian values and oratorical flourishes, Judge Drummond's speech was extensively reported in the press. He began by pointing out that Notman's social standing and level of education did not stand in the way of his doing right by the woman he had seduced. "In a country like ours there are no social distinctions. She was worthy of you in every respect.. She had beauty, education, intelligence, and judging from the manner in which she gave her testimony, and the tenderness with which she forbore to make damaging allusions towards yourself, she must have loved and cherished you in her heart." He did not wonder so much at the fact of a man yielding to temptation ("you were human"), as at the central enigma of the situation: "Why, when you had both of you so far fallen, did you not take her to your home, your heart, and to your bosom, and make her an Honourable woman and a happy wife?"

After Margaret's "first sad sin," Notman had led her into another even more grievous one. It made no difference that she was a willing party. Her desire to hide her shame was entirely understandable. The judge was clearly impressed by Margaret's background. His description of her family suggests that he had seen her parents. "A woman, brought up like her, by religious, by Puritan parents, themselves reared in the stern, unrelenting principles of old Puritanism; she, knowing that all she held dear in this world might be forfeited by the discovery of this, her frailty, – was it surprising if she was resolved to risk even her life rather than lose her reputation?" Robert had had little to lose, Margaret – he said – everything.

He now threw the entire book at Robert, calling abortion a murder not only of "the issue of your guilty love," but potentially as well of Miss Galbraith. It was a crime that was gaining ground and that struck "at the root of society and threaten[ed] to annihilate everything." He found it harrowing to talk of it but did it in order "to check the contagion" of a practice that had all too many proponents. "You had exhausted the lore of those immoral abominable publications, sent from American cities over our frontier, into our townships (for I regret to say that it is from the Eastern Townships these cases most frequently come to us), you had provided medicines for her, and to such an extent that you had told a man – a stranger – on your second interview with him that you had given the unhappy mother drugs enough to operate on a dozen ordinary girls."

The judge laid full responsibility of Alfred Patton's participation in the act at Robert's door. It was he who had applied to Dr. Patton for assistance and when the doctor initially assented, Robert had expressed a tepid note of regret in a letter from Toronto. The judge now reached the full height of his eloquence: "But soon afterwards we find you as determined as ever, and you induced this young man, this Dr. Patton, to proceed to extremities. What was there on that dread night in the room in the St. Lawrence Hall, what passed there during that dark and mysterious night, will perhaps never be known; but, on the morning following that night, that man, Dr. Patton, was found dead, poisoned by his own hand. He was stricken with remorse so deeply on thinking that he had caused her death, that he preferred to take a leap into eternity, to face his Creator, rather than stay here to face along with you the consequences of his evil-doing."

It had been the judge's original desire that the "sickening" details of the case be suppressed. But he had, he said, since changed his mind and come to approve of the wide ranging coverage of the trial. It would prove to be "a warning to all who may be tempted to crush out life, before it had entered the world.... I desire it to be understood that, nearly always, none but those abandoned men known as quacks will ever lend themselves to the crime in question, and also that it is almost impossible to effect it, except at the hazard of life."

He wished he could be more lenient than he was about to be "but presiding as I do over the first Criminal Court of the land, I would be failing to protect the morals of the future if I did not perform my very painful duty to my country and to my God, if I did not pronounce a very severe sentence upon you." He had gone to the unusual step of consulting his fellow judges, who agreed with the difficult course he was about to take. "I do not mention this to throw the responsibility in any part on them. I never shrink from its assumption. I sentence you to be imprisoned in the Provincial Penitentiary at Kingston for the space and term of ten years."

The sentence was breathtakingly harsh, clearly designed to be both a warning and a deterrent to others.

But Judge Drummond was not yet done. He had additional salt to rub into the wound. "You should thank God that your venerable father is no more, and that he does not survive to be shocked with the knowledge of your crime, and of its expiation.... May God help and console you! You once had, I know, a strong religious tendency. Throw yourself at the feet of your Creator, and weep over the misery you have inflicted on others, on yourself."

By the time Drummond reached the end of his speech, he had dissolved into histrionic sobs. His final overwrought words were, "I feel that I have done my duty."

Notman, said the *Gazette*, "received his sentence with much courage and composure, although he was very pale."

A tone of subdued solemnity permeated the *Gazette*'s front-page editorial the day after the sentence was passed. "The case has excited a more painful interest than anything in the records of crime that has occurred for a long time in this country." It expressed compassion and sorrow for the Notman, Galbraith, and Patton families, and even for Margaret Galbraith, who until then, it had characterized with scorn. She was to be as much pitied as blamed, the editorialist wrote, for – at the risk of her own life – she had tried to avert ruin for herself and "blasting distress" for her parents.

The paper could not come to grips with Dr. Patton's motivation. Perhaps he was overcome with pity for Margaret, perhaps it was "the bribe" paid him by Notman. But what had persuaded him when "he had the world before him in all its high hopes and bright colours…?"

The first step in his "vile deed" was prescribing medicine. The *Gazette* conceded that this measure did not actually pose a danger to the mother's life. But when it came to the use of instruments, "We are told that out of one hundred cases … sixty are fatal." How could the doctor have had such little regard for his patient's life with odds like this? But then he also had scant esteem for his own. "He knew, his death proves that he knew, that he was playing a game which if lost was an infamous fate on the scaffold."

The *Gazette* showed a firm grasp of the American abortion scene, and hoped that Judge Drummond was mistaken in thinking it was gaining ground locally. What particularly alarmed the *Gazette* was the spectre of a declining birthrate "in certain classes" among whom "few married women will consent to give birth to more than one or two children." This was code for the threat of the middle class being outnumbered by legions of poor but fecund French Canadians and Irish Catholics. Instead, the editorialist blamed the situation on selfish and frivolous women who abandoned their children to "hirelings," while they kicked up their heels in the ballroom or the theatre. It was a state of affairs "sufficient to call down the brimstone of Gomorrah."

In an editorial of April 30, the *Daily Witness* called the sentence of ten years "a terrible and ominous warning to seducers." It had been a long time since a case "of such importance to society" had come to trial, and regrettable as it was to have to have had to report it, exposing this crime to the public was of crucial importance. "There is but too much ground to believe that ... the frustrating of nature, even at the risk of life, and the commission of murder, is more common than we have heretofore suspected, or have been willing to believe." There was, however, cause for celebration that "no signs have yet appeared amongst us that in our married homes a numerous family is not still counted a joy and a crown of Honour to the parents." Again, attention was called to "the shameless writers and preachers of an evangel of sterility" in the United States.

The editorialist must have sent a chill down the spine of many a reader with the eerie eloquence of his conclusion: "On reviewing the history of the present case, it really seems as if Providence had interfered to suddenly shed a livid light upon these practices, and to make us aware of the presence of the secret wickedness amongst us. Had the remorse-struck and terrified Dr. Patton not rashly taken his own life, to escape from the thought of having, as he supposed, taken that of another, this offence too, like others, might have been hushed up, or remained totally undiscovered. But the knocking at the gate was too loud to be disregarded, his death startled us like a crack of thunder at early dawn, awaking the peaceful sleeper; and we were compelled, in the morning, to look upon the remains of the hideous spectacle which had been enacted during the stillness, and under cover of, the night."

The most revealing observations about the Notman case were published in the May 1868 issue of the *Canada Medical Journal*, a monthly periodical edited by Dr. George Fenwick and Dr. Francis Wayland Campbell. One of the brightest lights of the McGill medical establishment – an eccentric always late for appointments, who billed patients only when he needed funds – Dr. Fenwick was the best surgeon of his day in the city. Dr. Campbell we have already encountered in court, when he gave graphic testimony about the condition in which he found Margaret Galbraith, whose care he took over upon the death of Dr. Patton.

Referring to a new publication on the diseases of women by T. Gaillard Thomas, M.D., of New York, the authors expressed shock "that one of the most respectable newspapers of that city, one which finds its way into the first circles of society – contained in a recent issue no less than fifteen advertisements of well-known professional abortionists – men and women who make a business of infantile murder." Fenwick and Campbell felt that until recently they could congratulate themselves on Canada having escaped "being drawn completely into the current." However, they noted with feelings of profound regret "that at last, in Montreal, one of our profession was found willing to undertake the abominable business."

The authors went on to summarize the case. Like Drummond, they seemed impressed by Margaret Galbraith's conduct, saying that they believed the testimony she had given with evident reluctance. "Other witnesses gave evidence which completed the chain around the unfortunate prisoner. Notwithstanding most pathetic appeals to the jury, by two of the ablest criminal lawyers which Montreal possesses, he was found guilty...."

Though they endorsed the jury's verdict, "yet for all that we must add that we consider Judge Drummond has erred on the side of severity in the terrible sentence which he pronounced against the unfortunate prisoner." In their opinion, "the majesty of the law would have been satisfied with a sentence of from five to seven years." But, even with their softer approach to sentencing, the doctors deemed Notman's crime deserving of harsher punishment than the terms Judge Drummond had meted out to hardened and violent offenders at the same session of the court.

The most provocative section of the article dealt with a question that was never raised during the trial: the frequency with which physicians were called on to act as Dr. Patton had done.

> We are no apologists for the seducer, or the aider and abettor in the abominable crime of abortion, yet we know it for a fact that more than one person in Montreal occupying a position equal to that of Notman's would have been today in a position similar to his had it not been for the warning given them of the crime they intended to commit, by the persons they sought to make the principal offenders.... [T]here are few medical men, in Montreal at all events, who have not been at least once in their lives solicited to procure an abortion, the person so soliciting having no idea that he ran any risk

worth speaking about. A medical man does however, know not only the risk he runs, should he consent, but likewise is in a position to know the danger which he who 'counsels and procures' is liable; not only is it his duty therefore to refuse to become a party to any such crime but likewise to warn those soliciting him to desist."

Notman's misfortune, Fenwick and Campbell implied, was simply in getting caught. They went one step further, stating their regret that the law did not have the power "to prosecute mothers who in the crime of abortion, attempt to hide their shame." They hoped that the publicity attendant on the trial would result in "banishing from our country this moral cancer which was slowly eating its way into this and other cities of the Dominion."

CHAPTER SIXTEEN

"The Convict Notman"

"This morning at 8:30, the convict Robert Notman was removed from the common gaol here to the Penitentiary, Kingston, to undergo his term of imprisonment for 10 years. He was in charge of High Constable Bissonnette, and went by rail from the Bonaventure Station." – *Montreal Gazette*

AT KINGSTON STATION on the late afternoon of May 15, 1869, High Constable Adolphe Bissonette unbolted the sealed car that held the Provincial Penitentiary's complement of criminals newly sentenced by the Court of Queen's Bench in Montreal. Manacled to each other in pairs, Josephine Narbeau, Clemence Beauvais, Amable Gagnon, Thomas Sye, George Wilson, and Robert Notman hobbled down the stairs. Guards from the penitentiary snapped shackles around their ankles and urged them to mount the horse-drawn wagon awaiting them. The cart was lined with wooden benches with metal rings at their base. The guards leaned over to fasten the shackles to the rings. *Don't even think of getting away.*

Kingstonians barely gave the wagon a glance as it clip-clopped through the streets. A Loyalist town founded on the shores of Lake Ontario, Kingston was the home and riding of the prime minister, the same John A. Macdonald (by now knighted for his role as the architect of Confederation) photographed earlier in the decade at the Notman Studio. It had served as the capital of the United Canadas in the 1840s and was studded with some fine public buildings and gracious homes. But overall it was a rough-hewn industrial and marine town with teeming shipyards and sketchy bars. Convicts were one of its commonplaces.

The approach to the prison through the North Gate was appropriately forbidding – the entrance through an arch evoking Roman triumphal architecture. Low Tuscan columns supported a limestone pediment that symbolized society's victory over transgression.

Entering it, the Convict Notman could not but have felt a crushing despair.

And fear. This was the oldest and most infamous penitentiary of the Dominion. Its thirty-year history was steeped in corruption and blood. Greed and cruelty trumped the high-minded – if contradictory – ideals of its founders.

Inspired by the theories of the great British philanthropist John Howard, Kingston Penitentiary was Canada's first attempt at establishing a principled and humane correctional institution. Dreaming of becoming "a school of reform, where the idle will be usefully employed and the vicious reclaimed, to the good of themselves, and of society at large," it received its first prisoners in 1835.

The fact that its first warden flagrantly abused the unfortunates consigned to his care nipped these early ambitions in the bud. Over the course of fourteen years, Warden Henry Smith oversaw a reign of terror that featured punishments deemed outrageous even in an era that sanctioned the infliction of physical pain: the flogging of child convicts as young as eight years of age, bread-and-water rations, the use of thirty-five-pound yokes, and imprisonment in "the box" – a species of upright coffin. In 1848, Smith was suspended and eventually dismissed following a public inquiry headed by George Brown of the Toronto *Globe*. Brown's lengthy report decried the "revolting inhumanity" characterizing the institution.

Smith's successor, the soldier, politician, and public servant Donald Aeneas MacDonell, was fifty-six when he took over, and was still at the helm upon the arrival of the Convict Notman twenty years later. A veteran of both the War of 1812 and the 1837-38 rebellions, MacDonell had also served as a justice of the peace and a member of the provincial assembly. Though his administration was more benign than his predecessor's, MacDonell had become increasingly frail and lax with the years. By the time Notman arrived he was leaning heavily on his Deputy Warden, John Flanigan.

As laid down by the compendious list of the prison's *Rules and Regulations*, the day-to-day control of guards, keepers, watchmen, and convicts fell largely to Flanigan. He was to "examine the locks, levers and gratings of the cells and gates, fire arms and equipment of the Guards, and see that they have a proper supply of ammunition."

He was also to be a kind of super snoop, "constantly moving about the yard and places of labour, without previous notice, to see that the subordinate officers are vigilant and attentive in performance of their respective duties, and that the convicts are diligent, orderly and industrious, and do not talk or communicate with each other." A former butcher and military man, Flanigan had entered politics as an alderman and served as Kingston's mayor between 1854 and 1858. Judging by his childish handwriting and the uneven punctuation of his reports, he was a man of mean education and little culture. This did not hold him back from acquiring a considerable fortune, the tangible proof of which was a baronial holding with a grand name. Framed by fourteen acres of gardens and lawns, Eldon Hall was a villa in the Picturesque style erected on Flanigan's stately 120-acre farm. Its architect was the best of the local stable of architects, William Coverdale, who was also responsible for much of the design of the penitentiary and of its sister institution, the Rockwood Asylum for the Criminally Insane.

Among Flanigan's responsibilities as deputy warden was the reception of new inmates. "He shall superintend the cleansing and clothing of them according to the regulations of the Institution," stated the rules. "He shall take their height, weight, and description."

The wagon transporting the convicts from Montreal veered off King Street at the North Gate, making its first stop at the women's prison, where the two female prisoners were handed over to the matron. It then headed for the location designated for receiving male prisoners, where Flanigan and the Clerk of the penitentiary were waiting for them. (After 1900, this was the well-appointed office of the Chief Keeper, but no one today knows the precise setting in 1868.)

Flanigan barked out a series of questions at the new men; the Clerk entered their responses in a thick, oversized ledger.

Name?

–Robert Notman, sir.

State?

–State… sir?

Yes, *state*! Be you a married man or a bachelor?

–Widower, sir.

Age?

–Thirty-one, sir.

Trade?

–Photographer.

The Clerk, astonished, dropped his pen. He was used to inscribing occupations such as Labourer, Miller, Tailor, Bartender, Farmer, Sailor, Barber. But photographer? That was a first.

Can you read?

–Yes, sir.

Can you write?

–Yes, sir.

One of the ways in which the men were to be reformed at Kingston was through education. Child prisoners and illiterate young convicts were to be taught by a schoolmaster. At the discretion of the warden, the same teacher might devote time to the schooling of adults in accordance with their work schedule.

Where were you born?

–Scotland, sir.

What is your religion?

–Presbyterian.

The answers to the rest of the questionnaire the Deputy Warden dictated to the Clerk without resorting to the input of the prisoner. Notman stood five feet ten inches tall, had a fair complexion, light blue eyes, and brown hair. He was from the district of Montreal, had been sentenced to a term of ten years by the Honourable Justice Drummond at the Court of Queen's Bench on April 29. His crime was "counselling, procuring & commanding a person to administer a noxious thing with intent to procure a miscarriage."

Oh, how sick Robert Notman must have been of the sound of that oft-repeated mouthful. But this was not the time for contemplating his crime or his sorrows.

7108. He had been assigned his number.

A barber stepped up and sheared off his moustache with a few crude snips, and then applied himself to his skull, cropping it close. The man gestured to a nearby tub of disinfectant solution, miming the act of dousing the head. Another inmate measured him up quickly for a uniform. Soon a runner appeared with a pair of hobnail boots manufactured at the penitentiary shoe shop and a pile of heavy cotton canvas garments: underwear, a singlet, and the same odd baggy suits sported by the other convicts. It consisted of a waist-length buttoned jacket and ill-fitting long pants. Several features made the costume distinctive: both jacket and trousers were two-tone, blue on the right side, white on the left. His number was stamped over his heart, the letters K. P. adorned his back. Judging by the appearance of the other inmates, he must look like a poor relation of the harlequin clown that had so amused audiences at performances of the Theatre Royal back at home.

Once each man was catalogued and garbed, Flanigan ceased shouting. It was a short respite. As an old man shuffled into the room, the Deputy Warden roared the new convicts to attention. They were to stand when in the presence of Warden MacDonell.

In a barely audible voice the old man instructed them to heed his words carefully. He was about to read them the rules and regulations – these words he pronounced with portentous emphasis – of the Provincial Penitentiary. They must abide by them to the letter. Any violation of the same would result in appropriate punishment. Again, that ominous emphasis.

> The Convicts must observe strict silence. They must not laugh nor hold communication with each other, by word, sign, or any other manner: neither will they be permitted to speak to any of the Officers of the prison, except upon such matters as relates [sic] to their work; they must not stare at any person, nor will they be allowed to speak to a stranger, or receive anything from him.

The rule of silence cut to the heart of both the British and American prison reform movements of the early nineteenth century. The old European prisons that had so shocked John Howard were characterized by large communal day and night rooms, rife with filth and disease, and harbouring hardened criminals cheek by jowl with naïve first-timers. Reformers were divided over solutions to these problems. Some believed in strict single-cell isolation of all inmates whether at work or rest. Others – and this was the regime adopted at Kingston – were partial to communal arrangements for work, eating, and worship, and to individual cells for sleeping. It was an article of faith that a strictly administered rule of silence would prevent the corruption of the relatively innocent by the roughest elements. It would also encourage serious soul-searching by prisoners, reflection on their sins, and repentance of the same. This belief was embedded in the very name of the institution, the root of "penitentiary" being "penitence."

There were several corollaries to the rule of silence. Convicts were to make no noise or otherwise disrupt religious services, which were held daily, except for Sunday when they occurred twice. If they must speak to their overseers it must be strictly limited to the subject of work. Likewise to the surgeon, only about health. With the chaplains, only about spiritual affairs. However, to the warden they might speak about other subjects. This left the way clear for informers to snitch into the topmost ears.

There were a great many rules relating to cells: detailed instructions about the manner in which convicts were to cooperate in being secured within them, as well as the need to keep them clean and free of damage. One can imagine the stupefying effect of hearing these rules about the release and setting of levers before even having seen the physical plant.

Built on a radial plan featuring a central observation area connecting four three-storey wings beneath a classical dome, the penitentiary was designed in such a way that the rows of cells were easy to supervise. Writes architectural historian Jennifer McKendry, "'Avenues of Inspection' for the guards were inserted into the narrow corridors between ranges of cells.... An inmate could never be certain when he was being observed. The lack of opportunity to converse and thus form friendships drove a number of inmates mad, and they formed a ready-made clientele for the new Rockwood Asylum for the Criminally Insane.... The situation was a sad reflection on how easily reformers' theories could produce results opposite to their humane goals."

The cells themselves were minuscule to the point of provoking claustrophobia – twenty-nine inches wide by eight feet long. They faced inward toward the centre of the building and had no natural light. Critics referred to them as "pigeon-holes." A defender of the plan retorted: "The occupant had ample room to dress and undress, turn around, lie down, stand or sit, and the lengthened space for walking back and forth. And what more does he need? He would not occupy more space if he had it."

Huge chunks of time were spent in these pigeon cells. In the summer, from six at night until dawn inmates were confined to them in sweltering heat. Fall through March when the men were let out only during the short daylight hours, the dampness and cold penetrated their bones. Sundays were the worst because the bulk of the day was spent confined to the cells. As one of Robert's fellow convicts put it succinctly, "Rather work two days then lie over on Sunday. Confinement on Sunday [is the worst punishment.]"

The bells rang constantly. An outer safety bell tolled for opening the prison in the morning and securing it at night. An inner bell with a different timbre chimed the daily rhythms of rising, washing, dressing, worship, eating, and retiring for sleep. Until you learned to tune it out, the cacophony kept you perpetually on edge.

What were the inmates doing when they were inside their cells – pacing like caged beasts rehashing the same stale thoughts? *Would I be free now, had Mag only destroyed my letters? Why oh why did Alfred take the prussic acid? Why did I say what I did to that wretch Robert Murray?*

I shall go mad, perfectly mad. I shall be fodder for the Asylum.

Dear God, sweet Jesus, help me, help me. I am heeding Judge Drummond's words. On my knees, I return to Thee in abject penitence. I shall taste again the sweet spirituality of my youth. I shall be the perfect prisoner. I will obey every rule to the letter. I will be so exemplary as to earn myself a pardon.

Pardon was the great white hope of the good convict. "There is not a long sentenced man here who does not think he will get pardoned and as he has that hope he behaves himself well," said one Walter Jones on his release. Indeed, George Wilson, the British soldier whose trial for the killing of his officer during a drunken haze ran concurrently with Notman's, was pardoned seven years into the life sentence Drummond had decreed for him.

In the vastly detailed statistics kept by the Provincial Penitentiary, the names of certain prisoners blaze a red trail marked by public floggings with the so-called "Cats," bread-and-water rations, and confinements to the "Dark Cell," or to solitary. Not so Robert Notman. He was a model inmate, keeping a low profile. With the exception of his early years as a Sunday school teacher, it was the only time in his life that he was a model anything. Although his career in the penitentiary would prove to be exceptional, he surfaces a scant four times in the institution's records.

On May 16, the day after his arrival, Warden MacDonell noted in his official Journal that he had "ordered the Deputy Warden to see Convict Nottman [*sic*] at oven sent to The Foundry, and up to the [care?]... of the Surgeon and to be sent before him."

MacDonell wrote a flowery, nearly illegible script characterized by elaborate loops and flourishes. This cryptic entry suggests that Notman had been re-assigned from the kitchen to the penitentiary foundry, and suffered some injury there. Frustratingly, the information does not cross check with the surgeon or hospital's records from which Notman's name is entirely absent.

When next mentioned eight months later on December 12, he was written up with two others in the Punishment Register. Guard Absalom Johnson reported to the warden that Carter Mason, James Wall, and Robert Notman had committed the offence of talking in the dining hall. Mason owned up to having done so, Wall protested that he had "told Mason to be quiet." Both of them were admonished by MacDonell, but Notman protested his innocence. The warden believed him and left him alone.

While paramount as policy, the rule of silence was virtually unenforceable in practice, and broken all the time. No amount of scrutiny by the guards could catch every wink or gesture. Six hundred men in close proximity will always find ways of communicating.

Work was a possible way of anchoring sanity, but much depended on the nature and integrity of one's overseers. The penitentiary was a large enterprise spread out over a 200-acre site that included a ten-acre main compound, a series of stone quarries, and a farm. Prisoners were employed in shoe, carpentry, tailoring, blacksmith, stone cutting, and foundry workshops. They were also assigned to the penitentiary farm, hospital, kitchen, bakery, stables, and laundry.

Additional gangs worked off-site at the quarry, in construction on the railway line, and in maintenance of the perimeter walls of the institution.

Almost a year to the day that Dr. Patton aborted Margaret Galbraith at the St. Lawrence Hall, a Halifax newspaper carried a surprising short item from Montreal.

> Robert Notman's mother has petitioned His Excellency the Governor General for the liberation of her son, serving in the Kingston Penitentiary a ten years' term to which he was sentenced in April 1868.
> –*Halifax Evening Reporter*, February 20, 1869

Janet Notman, widow of William Senior, whom Robert had deemed at the time of his father's death on the verge of expiring herself, was trying to come to his rescue. He would have had no way of knowing because communication with the outside world was one long saga of frustration.

For the first year of his sentence, according to a long-standing rule, inmates were not allowed to write their own letters. Paper and pen were considered contraband and candles were forbidden in cells, which in any case held no furniture that would accommodate writing. Incoming mail was vetted in the warden's office. As for outgoing mail, a most unsatisfactory system existed: a form letter filled out by a guard appointed to this task, who would tick off on the prisoner's behalf a number of rote options, such as "Is quite well, etc.," or "Anxious to hear from you." Book 10 of the Convicts Letter Register contains the following extract from March 31, 1869, filled out for Robert by a Mr. P. Bell: "To Mrs. Mr Notman 'Health is good, received your letters regularly, etc.'" Presumably this was addressed to Janet Notman and meant to be shared with William.

The penitentiary Liberation Books (which catalogued at the time of their release prisoners' frank appraisals of life within the institution) are rife with complaints about Bell, the unpopular guard of the chapel and lazy librarian, much resented by the inmates. "Mr. Bell was a very disagreeable man in the position he held. If a convict asked him for a book or to write a letter he would give a very insulting answer. The system of having Mr. Bell write the convicts' letters was very objectionable."

In May 1869 – exactly one year into Robert Notman's sentence – Prime Minister Sir John A. Macdonald appointed a new warden. A sea change was about to take place at the penitentiary. Indefatigable and punctilious, only by comparison to the administrators before him, can James Moir Ferres be deemed a true reformer. That title was merited by his own successor, John Creighton, a humanitarian who improved conditions for his charges immeasurably. Still, Creighton judged that Ferres, during his short tenure (he died within a year of taking office), "greatly advanced the cause of humanity and civilization among the ... inmates."

From the moment that he took over from MacDonell, Ferres was the proverbial new broom sweeping clean. His Journal and Liberation Book entries are chock full of details about prison life written in a schoolmaster's clear script. In fact, he began his career as a teacher after coming to Montreal from Scotland in 1833 at the age of twenty. By temperament partisan and combative, he was an aggressive Tory who found his true calling in journalism and politics. In the 1840s he was by turn editor of the Montreal *Herald* and of the *Gazette*, where his incendiary opposition to the Rebellion Losses Bill of 1849 incited the English merchants of the city to their crazed action of burning down the Parliament buildings in April of that year. (He had called the bill "a nefarious attempt at robbery" of the Anglos by "an insignificant French nationality in a corner of Canada.") As a result, he was actually arrested for arson, though soon released on bail and never prosecuted.

When the *Gazette* changed ownership in the 1850s, Ferres tried his hand as a parliamentarian but found the experience unsatisfactory. In 1861 he began to serve on a newly created Board of Inspectors of Asylums and Prisons. Eight years later he accepted the post of warden at Kingston.

Ferres moved quickly to centralize the affairs of the prison under his own control. Within days of taking office he was putting Henry Horsey, the penitentiary architect, on notice as to who was the boss: "I desire to know every thing which you yourself know or which is mentioned to you by others relative to the Prison and its interests."

One of his first acts was to request from Hewitt Bernard, the Deputy Minister of Justice, the accelerated discharge of one Phidime Bond. Ferres explained that Bond was a "well behaved prisoner" who, if not released before winter freeze up, would have to travel on foot through wilderness to get to his home in the Gaspé. The warden requested a grace period of six weeks on his behalf, so that Bond could catch the last steamer for the Bay of Chaleurs. This decent and compassionate gesture was typical of Ferres's attitude to a compliant prisoner. (One of his improvements was to grant permission to well-behaved literate inmates to write their own letters, for instance.)

Faced with defiance, however, he was ferocious and implacable. His chief *bête noire* was one Narcisse Bernard (a.k.a. Francis Murat), an illiterate labourer and toughened recidivist from Montreal, whom Ferres dubbed "the greatest blackguard in the Prison for years." In the fall of 1869 Bernard went on a rampage during which he forced himself into the cell of another convict with – according to Ferres – "some evil object" in mind. "Insolent and unsubdued," Bernard resorted to tearing bricks out of the walls and beating up the guards. It took a full two weeks of public floggings, sojourns in the "Dark Cell," and of being chained to the floor in solitary, before Ferres could write triumphantly in his journal: "This morning … he promised good behaviour and I took the chain off him."

It has been estimated that up to twenty-five percent of the inmates of the penitentiary at the time were mentally ill, although few of them were diagnosed as such. When they were, they were handed off to the local asylum for the criminally insane for confinement, though not for treatment. Whether Narcisse Bernard went mad because of his repeated incarcerations or whether he ended up in prison because he was insane, the job fell to Ferres's successor, John Creighton, to have him committed to the Rockwood Asylum in May 1870, from where he escaped in November 1872.

As vigilant and demanding of his underlings as he was of his convicts, from dawn late into the night Ferres was wedded to his job. His daily tours of inspection of the wings and shops turned up myriad examples of petty theft and negligence by guards and foremen who had flourished under his predecessor. Ferres moved swiftly to fire corrupt guards and replace them with better appointments.

The Warden's combination of fierce discipline and strict honesty won the grudging respect, confidence, and eventual loyalty of the inmates, especially after he cracked down on the staff of the Protestant Chapel. Religious worship was an integral part of prison life, and was intended to be a prime tool of rehabilitation. In an age of faith, even hardened and brutalized men believed in the divine. But even the simplest among them could see right through the Reverend Mulkins. Ferres noted right away that he was treating his position as a sinecure and was universally scorned by his flock. ("He did not appear to care more than to put in his time and get his pay," one convict put it succinctly.)

The warden addressed the problem to the highest authority, the Prime Minister. Soon Mulkins was on an extended leave of absence. Ferres replaced him with the sincere and conscientious Reverend Mulvany, who became instantly popular with the inmates.

October 1869 brought a moment of rare cohesiveness to the entire prison population. Word came down from on high that the penitentiary would be graced by a visit from Lord Lisgar, the Governor General, and by Prince Arthur, a younger brother of the Prince of Wales who had opened Montreal's Victoria Bridge nine years earlier. Ferres received his instructions from Sir John A. "that every thing should be in order," but concluded that since "we have every thing in perfect order at all times," it was best to look natural, and "they should see us in our actual *working dress.*" He requested advice from Flanigan, Chief Keeper McCarthy, and the matron of the Women's Prison – "their experience of the Prison being more intimate than mine as yet" – as to who might best deserve a pardon, if it so moved the Governor General to mark the visit by an exercise of royal clemency.

To pay tribute to the illustrious guests, convicts were set to work erecting a decorative arch on the prison grounds. Other men struggled to repair a boiler for a broken furnace. "The men at the Arch were out until dark. The men at the Boiler till 7 o'clock," Ferres recorded on October 6. "They all worked with as much heartiness and zeal as if they have been earning large wages." As a reward, he ordered them all "a white bread ration and the Boiler men meat in addition."

Thursday, October 7 dawned to beautiful sunshine and at nine o'clock, Lord Lisgar arrived with his entourage, along with the mayor of Kingston "and other leading gentlemen of the City." The Governor General expressed satisfaction with all that he saw, but alas, the nineteen-year-old royal was absent "in consequence of the fatigue he had undergone during the past three days and nights." Later that day, a lucky few caught a glimpse of him, as he drove past the gates with a volunteer cavalry escort on their way to inspect the asylum.

The prisoners having conducted themselves as model citizens during the exercise and having behaved irreproachably two nights running, Ferres gave them a congratulatory speech on Friday morning and remitted all punishments.

Eight days later on October 15, seemingly out of the blue but in fact a consequence of a protracted legal battle, Ferres received a telegram from Bernard Devlin, stating that an order had been issued to transport Robert Notman from Kingston to Montreal. The High Constable was on his way to fetch him.

CHAPTER SEVENTEEN

The Appeal

BERNARD DEVLIN HAD NEVER given up on his client and had kept
on petitioning on his behalf. In the spring of 1869, he had renewed
his application to the Court of Queen's Bench – Judge Monk then
presiding – that the case be heard again on the ground that a jumbled and incorrect version of the indictment printed in the *Herald* newspaper had been given to the jury after they were seques-
tered. Making favourable noises, Judge Monk held out hope that
after consulting with his colleagues "they would probably be able to
come to some understanding on the matter."

In the meantime, the Convict Notman was in the dark about the
legal machinations of the defence team. On September 21, after a five-
month campaign, a victorious Devlin obtained a writ of error staying
the conviction of the prisoner for the now famous crime of "feloniously counselling, procuring and commanding a person to administer a noxious thing with intent to procure a miscarriage." The *Gazette*
speculated that Devlin would make an application for bail after Notman's release from Kingston by means of a writ of habeas corpus. (A
writ of habeas corpus typically commands a prison warden to surrender a prisoner to the court that had sentenced him and is a way
of contesting the legality of a confinement. It can be used to oblige a
judge to grant bail and reopen a case.) In Notman's case the implication was that the sojourn in the penitentiary had been unlawful.

Alas for Devlin, when on Saturday, October 2, 1869 he brought
his application to the Court of Queen's Bench, he once again came
head-to-head with his old nemesis, Judge Drummond. Drummond
gave a foretaste of what was to come: he postponed proceedings
until the following week.

On Monday, when Devlin made his motion, the lawyer for the
Crown, Thomas W. Ritchie, offered the ludicrous opinion that it
was not within the jurisdiction of the court to issue the writ to the
penitentiary, since it was situated in Ontario. Devlin treated this

comment with the contempt it deserved. "It would be strange if this court had not jurisdiction over a prison where its own prisoners were sent. The penitentiary was not for Ontario only, but equally for Quebec." His Honour again deferred his decision.

By the next day Judge Drummond had hit on a new way to stall. He reminded the court that there had originally been five indictments against Notman, though he had only been tried on one of them. He refused to rule on habeas corpus until the Crown informed him whether it intended to proceed with the outstanding indictments. Thomas Ritchie equivocated, hiding behind the authority of Attorney General Gédéon Ouimet, whom he said he would first have to consult. Drummond advised Ritchie instead to seek out T. K. Ramsay, who was conversant with the case.

Useless for Devlin to protest that the Crown's intentions about the indictments were "utterly immaterial." His Honour had not sentenced Robert Notman to ten years in order to see him reinstated to his former status after a measly seventeen months. And though Drummond promised a decision for the following day, he shelved the matter until October 14. When he finally did pronounce, it was to say that a writ of habeas corpus did not apply in the case of a felony. "It is clear," he added, "that the demand to admit the prisoner to bail is premature. The only action which the Court can take is to send the prisoner back to jail." He suggested that Devlin withdraw his motion and replace it with a petition "in accordance with the statute, to have the prisoner brought before this Court."

In this game of cat and mouse, the judge had the upper hand and Devlin knew it. While continuing to maintain that the writ of habeas corpus applied, he nevertheless agreed to withdraw his motion and the following day requested permission to have the prisoner Robert Notman brought before the court. His strategy was to first prise Notman out of the penitentiary, then get bail for his client and launch an appeal.

The judge granted the required permission but bided his time. A telegram was sent to Warden Ferres on October 15.

In a moment of striking déjà vu, on Thursday, October 22 at eleven o'clock in the morning, Robert Notman once more stood at the bar in front of Judge Drummond. Amid a storm of hammering emanating from below, where repairs were being made to the heating system, His Honour intoned the five indictments that had been brought against the prisoner a year and a half earlier. The first two were almost identical to each other: "For feloniously administering a certain noxious thing with intent to procure a miscarriage," and "For feloniously administering a noxious thing with intent to procure a miscarriage." The third was the infamous one on which he had already been tried, convicted, and sentenced. The last two had to do with the use of means, i.e. instruments, to bring on a miscarriage. In the former of these, Notman was charged as a principal in the second degree, in the latter of "counselling, procuring and commanding" Dr. Patton to use such instruments.

In highfaluting legalese the judge allowed that though Notman had been tried, convicted, and sentenced on one of the charges, on September 21, 1869 "a writ of error was issued against the said sentence whereby the conviction was stayed." Consequently, it was his duty to place Robert Notman "in the same state and conditions in which he was when the said sentence was pronounced." Since Notman remained untried on the four other indictments against him, the judge commanded the High Constable – who continued to have custody of the prisoner – to take him back to the Montreal Common Gaol where he had been residing since his return to the city. Notman was to be delivered to the custody of the Keeper of the Gaol "to await the decision of the Court sitting in Appeal and Error upon the writ of error issued against the said sentence …, and to stand his trial upon the said indictments upon which the said Robert Notman has not yet been tried, or to be otherwise discharged in due course of law."

In the parlance of a Monopoly game, "Go directly to jail. Do not pass go. Do not collect $200." Instead of being granted bail, Robert Notman was back where he had started. Conditions inside the Montreal jail were generally worse than those he had left behind. Upon their liberation, Kingston convicts were always asked to compare the penitentiary to other jails with which they were familiar. From Narcisse Bernard down, they had choice words for the Montreal institution. "The common gaol is worse than the penitentiary." "Bad place." "Morals will not be improved there." Bernard said, "It was harsher in labour than this is."

Since Notman was awaiting trial again, he was probably not put to labour, which must have made the days excruciatingly long and boring. Rations were skimpy, but as a technically untried prisoner, he was permitted visitors on Fridays between ten and twelve in the morning, and one and four in the afternoon. Because of his status as untried, his friends were allowed to bring him food, clothing, and such books as were approved by the chaplain.

As the days and weeks stretched out, his visitors must have reassured him that his cause was being advanced. At last early in the new year, there was good news. Notman's appeal for bail was finally heard, fortunately for him before Mr. Justice Monk not Judge Drummond. "Notman will be released on bail at three o'clock," reported the *Gazette* on January 3, 1870, "and there will be a new trial at the next term of the Court of Queen's Bench." The bail terms were interesting. "Mr. W. Notman gives bail in $2,000, Dr. Godfrey, $2,000, and the prisoner himself in $4,000." Robert Notman, it appears, was not an impoverished man. In today's dollars, the amount of his bail would run to between $120,000 and $135,000 – and $4,000 was a tidy sum. Dr. Godfrey was Robert T. Godfrey, M.D., physician and surgeon, whose home and office were located at the corner of St. Catherine Street and McGill College Avenue. A professor at the Bishop's Medical School, Godfrey was likely a close family friend.

Robert must have found life back at 3 Eliot Terrace while out on bail, a mixed blessing. The absence of clanging bells, the luxury of a feather pillow and warm quilt, the flavours of his mother's cooking were surely a great boon, but he must also have had to contend with meeting a constant reminder of his troubles in Janet Notman's anxious gaze. Annie, his little girl – not yet six years old – likely shrank from him as from a stranger. He had been gone for almost two years from her life; surely she had gathered an inkling of his whereabouts and wickedness.

What was he to do with himself? Polite society gave him a wide berth. In Toronto around this time a campaign was being waged against seducers, encouraging "the heads of respectable families peremptorily to exclude" these licentious men from their homes and tables. The mores of Montreal could not have been been much different, especially in the case of a recently convicted felon. Resuming his business on Peter Street as a commission agent was hampered by his notoriety, and it is unlikely that William – whose reputation had not improved because of the association between them – could use him at the studio.

He lived under a cloud, alternately dreading the next appearance in court, since it might put an end to his freedom, and yet looking forward to it too, as it might just make a free man of him once and for all. He had to know that his options were limited: either the appeal would be turned down, or – if it was successful – he might well be tried on the four outstanding indictments. It would hardly be surprising if he slid into depression or took to drink. He had been thrown out of his church years ago. Perhaps he was able to join some marginal congregation and obtain a measure of succour there.

By the time his case was heard by the Appeal Side of the Court of Queen's Bench, Robert Notman had stopped being front-page news. In the early days of September 1870, the papers were agog with the momentous advance of the Prussians into French territory during the Franco-Prussian War. Maps were splashed across the pages of dense coverage beneath headlines such as "THE BATTLE BEFORE SEDAN," "TERRIBLE STRUGGLE," "SCENES ON THE BATTLEFIELD," "DEFEAT OF FRANCE AT EVERY POINT," and "FRIGHTFUL SLAUGHTER." The fate of the brother of the photographer was consigned to small print in the back.

On September 7, Robert Notman, "the plaintiff in error," stood before Chief Justice Jean-François-Joseph Duval, Mr. Justice René-Édouard Caron, Mr. Justice Lewis Thomas Drummond, Mr. Justice William Badgley, and Mr. Justice Samuel Cornwallis Monk of the Court of Queen's Bench. Hope and fear warred within his chest, as he hung upon every technical syllable of their considered decision read by the Honourable Chief Justice.

He was informed that they had heard out Bernard Devlin, Esquire, on his behalf, and also the Honourable Attorney General, Gédéon Ouimet, on behalf of the Queen. They had reviewed the records, proceedings, and judgment of his case, and had given all the aforesaid their "mature deliberation." They were now in a position of full comprehension and were able to conclude "that there is no error either in the records or proceedings aforesaid, or in the giving of the Judgment aforesaid."

With Judges Badgley and Monk dissenting from the decision of the other three, "therefore it is considered and adjudged by this Court that the Judgment aforesaid be in all things affirmed & stand in full force and effect and that the Sheriff of the District of Montreal, present here, in Court do re-deliver the said Robert Notman … into the custody of the Warden of the Kingston Penitentiary there to undergo the unexpired term of his imprisonment in the said Penitentiary in pursuance of the Judgment aforesaid."

His extended legal roller coaster ride thudded to a halt. He was not to be reprieved. He was to be catapulted all the way back to Kingston immediately. The Sheriff stood by to take him away.

CHAPTER EIGHTEEN

The Disappearing Act

ROBERT NOTMAN NEVER arrived back at Kingston Penitentiary. There is no entry in any Liberation Book of the date of his discharge, or his answers to the questionnaire the Warden would have read him had he served out his sentence. Thus we have no way of knowing whether he thought his cell too narrow, or the food inadequate, or the meat served in the summer sometimes a little tainted. We are equally ignorant about his familiarity with any plots being hatched among the prisoners, or about his opinion as to the most effective method of enforcing discipline being the Cats, or confinement in a dark solitary cell with privation of food. He would have been asked as well if he planned to continue his trade as a photographer, and if he felt that his stint in the penitentiary had reformed his character. And just as there is no knowing the answers to these putative questions, there is none to one he would never have been asked: what deal was reached by him or on his behalf with which authorities?

All we have to go on in the official record is a notation of the date of his discharge in the Prisoners' Record Book for 1843-1890. Given as October 18, 1869, three days after Warden Ferres received the telegram from Montreal, it was probably inscribed much after the fact. In the narrow column of the register entitled "Remarks," where it was customary to give the reasons for a prisoner's departure (remission, pardon, death, suicide), the words "Removed by Order of Court" have been squeezed. While that was certainly true of Notman's surprising exit in October 1869, there is no trace of the order of the court that sent him back to Kingston eleven months later, nor of his being readmitted.

Did he give the Sheriff the slip? It would have been highly out of character for a model inmate such as he had been, and well nigh impossible for a fettered man. He would have been caught in no time.

A couple of generations after Notman's sojourn in the penitentiary, the birth-control activist and penal reformer Dr. Oswald

C. J. Withrow reported a common saying among inmates. Withrow had first-hand experience of "The Pen." In the late 1920s, he had served two and a half years of a seven-year sentence for performing an abortion, and subsequently wrote the compelling prison memoir, *Shackling the Transgressor.* According to him, the prisoners' maxim was "It is easier for a camel to go through the eye of a needle than for a rich man to enter Kingston Penitentiary." "Wealth," wrote Withrow, had the power "to mitigate sentences and effect releases." Stories abounded inside of wealthy men bribing their way out. This of course was both hearsay and long after Robert Notman's time. Besides, in his case if there was a bribe it had to do with keeping him from being returned to the penitentiary, not with getting him out.

But a deal there had to have been, whether money changed hands or not, because according to Notman Studio lore, by November 1870 Robert was managing a new branch in Halifax. In 1868-1869, taking advantage of the new business opportunities afforded by Confederation, William Notman was expanding his reach, and in quick succession opened studios in Ottawa, Toronto, and Halifax. It being his general practice to place a family member in charge of these outposts, the first candidate in Halifax was his brother James, who headed the enterprise between April 1869 and August 1870.

Both McAlpine's Halifax Directory for 1871-1872 and the Canadian census of 1871 corroborate Robert's presence in the city. McAlpine's gives his work place as 38 George Street, the studio address. The census lists him as boarding at 50 Creighton Street in district 196, West Halifax. The lodging appears to have been respectable, run by Mrs. Mary Shelnutt, age twenty-six, a widow, with the help of her twenty-two-year-old sister-in-law Eva, and a servant called Eliza Clemens, whom the census described as being a seventeen-year-old Baptist of African descent. There was one other boarder, a Presbyterian bookkeeper thirty-two years old and of Scottish descent.

Of the three Notman branches that Robert could be exiled to, Halifax was the farthest. It is quite likely that the terms of the mysterious agreement stipulated he never show his face again in Montreal.

There is a tantalizing entry penned in Warden Ferres's Journal on October 12, 1869, just days before he was sent the directive from the court in Montreal that began Robert's appeal process: "Received a letter from UnderSecy. of State directing Convict Henry Schram to be released on condition of banishing himself from the former Province of Canada for ten years. Obtained from him a writing to that effect and telegraphed the Under Secy. to know if I should release him...." This item suggests there were some unorthodox ways of leaving prison.

There is no similar document about Robert, whose situation in any case was different from Schram's because he was outside and not in the penitentiary. Who could have authorized, even sub rosa an overturning of the decision of an appeals court? It would have had to have been someone at the very top, someone to whom a private appeal could be made by William Notman.

William Notman had been photographing Sir John A. Macdonald since 1862, well before the latter's prime ministership or knighthood. Intriguingly, there is a striking painted photograph of the great man taken at a Notman studio in 1869. Knees crossed and typically debonair, Macdonald posed with his elbow resting on a carved desk, a fringed ottoman on the floor at his right, and the Houses of Parliament – more than a little out of perspective – glimpsed through a window behind him. Both the Montreal studio and the Ottawa branch owned identical versions of the desk and the stool to facilitate artistic renditions in either location. The picture was almost certainly taken at the Ottawa branch and likely finished in the Montreal studio's art department which was more experienced at such work and had better artists.

Sir John A. had represented Kingston from his earliest days in politics and took keen interest in the affairs of the penitentiary. He was no champion of abortion. In a private letter of January 4, 1871, he wrote, "the practice saps the life blood of a nation and must be put down with a strong hand." But Macdonald had been a rake in his youth, and was sufficiently worldly to sympathize with someone of good family who had run afoul of the law. He had been born in Glasgow, where William and Robert grew up. Sir John A. was renowned for his flexibility and pragmatism. And he was never averse to contributions to the coffers of his party.

Be all that as it may, by 1873 Robert Notman's name was no longer listed in the Halifax directory. He would only return to Montreal in a coffin.

CHAPTER NINETEEN

"In the Streets and in the Broad Ways"

THE VILLAGE OF SOUTH STUKELY consists of a couple of crossroads and a few streets lined with a smattering of tidy houses. On a sultry day in August, a breeze stirs the great white heads of the hydrangeas in the front yards. A pretty stone church with a silver steeple perches on a nearby hillock. Silhouetted against the horizon loom dark clumps of spruce, pine, and cedar. To the east rises Mount Orford.

Small knolls and ponds dot the rolling country highway leading to a cemetery enclosed by a chain-link fence and gate. The angular, no-nonsense graveyard holds an array of nineteenth-century as well as more recent stones, the austere rows separated by ribbons of clipped lawn.

The Galbraith plot is located in ranges nine and ten.

Once upon a time, the granite monuments in honour of Archibald and five of his children lined up like soldiers at attention here. But when the porous stone began to crumble, a Galbraith descendant erected a square block of shiny marble to commemorate the six names.

Archibald Galbraith
1795 – 1872
Native of Dumbartonshire, Scotland
Also His Children
Robert 1855 – 1871
Helen 1845 – 1878
Margaret 1843 – 1879
Ann J. 1859 – 1880
William G. 1864 – 1865

Off to the side of the Galbraith plot, a visitor will spot a tiny grave that has been allowed to surrender to nature. On its eroded grey face, the outline of a sculpted lamb in a recessed niche is still discernible. Dropping to my haunches to read the worn letters, I am overcome with sorrow.

ROBERT

Only son of
Robert and Margaret

NOTMAN

Died February 15, 1877
Age 1 year 7 months

Suffer Little Children to come unto me

The two words that leap out at me are the "Robert" and the "Notman." I know who grieved this child so sorely. It is the woman who I have come to think of as "my Margaret." In her pain, she wanted the world to acknowledge that her precious baby was named both Robert and Notman, just like his father. And she needed to shout out for all to hear that she, too, was a Notman now.

But how had she become one? Who had found whom and when?

The woman who had been a celebrity at the trial of her lover nine years earlier, who had taken the stand at first in hysterics, then with increased confidence, and finally with the colossal brio to deny ever setting eyes on one of Montreal's most prominent physicians – *her* word against Dr. Duncan Campbell MacCallum's – this woman whose testimony was blazoned in the local papers, broadcast to the wind across the Dominion, and blown back to her native Scotland, this same woman whose secrets were fodder for both scandal-mongers and sanctimonious upholders of society's norms and mores, this woman craved nothing but anonymity for the rest of her life.

And yet she had her pride. She did not bury her toddler son anonymously in a pauper's grave. A beautiful little stone in a picturesque setting was one way to expiate the ignominious fate of that bloody bundle torn from her body by Dr. Patton at the St. Lawrence Hall, and whisked away by him in a bucket.

Another way to put all to rights was marriage.

* * *

Where Margaret Galbraith disappeared to and what she did after the trial may have been known to her closest confidantes, but if so they guarded her privacy. Almost all her secrets died with her. *Almost* all.

Though the Montreal newspapers announced Miss Galbraith's intention to sail to Scotland immediately after the end of the trial in the spring of 1868, no record has been found of her having returned to the British Isles. Three years later, the Canadian census of 1871 did not list her with the rest of her family in South Stukely. But if you look for her elsewhere in the Dominion in 1871, you will find her. You will find her in district 196, West Halifax, in the province of Nova Scotia, sub-district Portuguese Cove.

Margaret Galbraith – twenty-eight, born in Scotland, Presbyterian, of Scots descent – was quite distinct from the other members of the household counted by the census taker. It was headed by an illiterate fisherman, Benjamin Petepas, and his wife Sarah, both sixty-five, both born in Nova Scotia, both Catholic. Benjamin was of French extraction, and Sarah of Irish. Six other Petepases ranging in age from eight months to twenty-four years also lived there, along with an eighteen-year-old fisherman of Irish background named Garrett Bennan.

In 1871 Portuguese Cove, on the rugged Chebucto Peninsula, was enumerated in the same electoral district as 50 Creighton Street, home of the manager of the Notman Studio in Halifax, the widower Robert Notman. Did he send for her once he took up his post in Halifax in November 1870? Or did she follow him on her own initiative?

Who had found whom – and when?

Among the most haunting lines of the sublime *Song of Songs* are these: "I will rise now, and go about the city. In the streets, and in the broad ways I will seek him whom my soul loveth."

Just as the Convicts' Register at Kingston gave the reason for a prisoner's departure, the Students' Register of the McGill Normal School also provided a space to insert observations about the doings and whereabouts of its graduates. In the case of Margaret Galbraith, the word "Left" was first written in and then struck through

this "Remarks" column. Beneath the deleted item was inscribed the abbreviation for the United States of America: "U.S."

New York City was a megalopolis even back in the 1870s, a place where a man on the run could find anonymity and a woman with a past could wipe it clean. On March 19, 1873, Margaret Galbraith Notman gave birth to Robert Notman's daughter, Margaret Janet Notman, in Manhattan, New York City. The father's name in the official record is Robert Notman. The child was named after her mother, just as Margaret had been after hers. The baby's second name was Janet, for Robert's mother. Perhaps he was honouring her in the traditional way a loving son pays tribute. Perhaps he had a special debt to pay to the woman who had originally begun the process by which he was eventually freed from Kingston.

A child born in the spring of 1873 would have been conceived around June 1872. By then, for whatever reason, Halifax had become too hot for the ex-Convict Notman.

Little Robert, buried in South Stukely in 1877, had an older sister nicknamed "Daisy."

To ascertain whether they actually married or whether Margaret merely used the Notman name, I hired a genealogist. After conducting a thorough Internet search, my genealogist ruled out the British Isles and the Province of Quebec as possible sites. "I suspect that if there was a marriage it took place in the United States, most probably in the State of New York," he reported, adding that "the majority of Protestant Marriages for the state for the 19th century are not online."

On the other hand, some marriages celebrated in the state of New York are indeed to be found online. As is the one between one Robert Notman, clerk, born in Paisley, Scotland and son of William Notman and Janet Sloan, to Lily May Thompson Rankin, who in other data also figures as a dressmaker named Lydia Rankin. The date of the marriage was January 15, 1878, eleven months to the day after the death of little Robert, "*Only son of Robert and Margaret* NOTMAN".

It surely is no coincidence that a month after her husband's bigamous move, Margaret Galbraith Notman issued an outraged salvo of protest. By this time she and four-year-old Daisy were living in the Eastern Townships village of Stanstead Plain. Today Stanstead is so intrinsically linked to the border town of Derby Line, Vermont that the two share a historic library and opera house straddling the international boundary. The two communities were always intimately close, Stanstead having originally been settled by New Englanders in the late eighteenth century. As the last Canadian stop on the Quebec-Boston stagecoach route, it was a lively commercial centre and travellers' hub.

Margaret probably had good reason to return to Canada even before Robert's spectacular treachery. Living with him had been hard on his first wife, Annie Birks, as well. (There had been rumours even back then of other women, and vague, unsubstantiated stories of an illegitimate child.) But if she did leave New York where could she go? Surely not back to Montreal with its nightmarish associations. South Stukely? Archibald had died in 1872, and her mother had recently remarried and moved away from the village. In any case, Margaret's ties to Stukely were also too wrenching, her history notorious.

Stanstead was a better choice, even though it would be impossible to find anonymity there either. If Robert chose to visit her and the little ones or to bring them money, he could stay on the American side. In certain parts of town it only meant she had to cross from one side of the street to the other to be in the States.

But if he didn't visit, didn't provide support, how did she survive in Stanstead? Certainly not as a teacher. Generally, female teachers retired upon marriage. And both the Notman and Galbraith names would have struck alarm bells in Stanstead, where the local paper, the *Stanstead Journal*, had given wide play to the trial in 1868, highlighting details such as, "Miss Galbraith had been delivered of a child in the fourth or fifth month. The prisoner fully admitted his share in the matter to one Murray, an acquaintance of Miss Galbraith. The jury brought in a verdict of guilty."

In a prosperous town with a middle class that reaped profits from local factories and the granite quarries that were its mainstay, she might have cleaned houses, taken in washing, or dressed hair. Maybe she scrubbed the floors of the church and the manse, and pressed the snow-white surplice of the Anglican priest, George Thornston. Whatever she did, her little girl was an unobtrusive shadow by her side, seen but not heard, save perhaps for her murmurs to a rag doll fashioned by her mother.

How did word of the marriage of Robert to Lily/Lydia Thompson Rankin, the dressmaker, reach Stanstead? Evil news flies fast. Had not Judge Drummond extolled the virtues of communication by telegraph? But you didn't need to send a telegram. There was an excellent postal service. And plenty of wagging tongues. Even clerking away in obscurity in New York City, Robert Notman would forever remain an object of interest in Montreal and the Eastern Townships.

Margaret was well acquainted with the sour taste of bile in her gullet. She had dined on a steady stream of it for much of the past decade. But this extravagant duplicity by her avowed husband, the father of her children, was in a category of bitterness all its own. It burned in her chest. Despite her limited options, she responded with a clarion call that invoked the judgement of God.

Little Daisy had not yet been baptized. Perhaps Margaret was waiting for a propitious time, when it would be safe for Robert to return. Or perhaps she was planning to take Daisy to New York, to surprise him with the way she was turning into a bonny lass. What a simpleton she had been! What a patsy.

She resolved to stop living in limbo. No more waiting! She clutched the child to her breast, then with feverish speed dressed her in a white smock. In haste, she arranged a small Anglican service, for Margaret was a member of the Church of England now, never again darkening the door of a Presbyterian establishment. And afterwards the priest inscribed into the Church of England register of the Eastern Townships community of Stanstead Plain & Beebe-Plain, the following words:

Margaret Janet daughter of *Robert Notman*, Clerk, of New York U.S.A. & *Margaret his wife*, born on the nineteenth day of March eighteen hundred and seventy-three, was baptized on this tenth day of February eighteen hundred & seventy eight by me.
Geo. Thornston, Incumbent....

The witnesses were an Annie Smith, Margaret Notman, and one W. L. Tuck who stood proxy for Robert Notman.

Margaret Galbraith figures only twice more in the official record, on both occasions as Margaret Notman. On October 6, 1879, the Montreal *Daily Witness* ran a terse note: Died: "NOTMAN – at Stanstead, P.Q., on the 1st inst. Margaret Galbraith, wife of Robert Notman of the city of New York, age 36."

In the annals of South Stukely's silver steepled Anglican church – the landmark on the hill that you notice as you drive into the village today – the information imparted in the newspaper obituary assumes an even darker aspect. The words on the page – many of them scratched out, then reworked – have been penned with a thick, splotchy nib. The uneven handwriting is a gravedigger's.

Notman Buried Margaret Galbraith Notman
wife of Robert Notman of New York City US. Died
on the second day of October (at Stanstead) one thousand
eight hundred & Seventy nine & was Buried on the fourth
day of ... the same month & year.
>   By me
>   J.W. Garland

A.D. Garland, A.E.G. Montgomery Witnesses

No cause of death is given.

Can you die of a broken heart? In addition to Robert's disloyalty, other blows rained down upon Margaret. Her sister Helen died in the spring of 1878 at the age of thirty-three. Margaret would have travelled from Stanstead for the funeral and later knelt by the grave of her little son, pondering the ways of God. She would also have paid her respects to her father Archibald, the "Puritan," that "Native of Dumbartonshire," who had so stalwartly lent her his protection during her public agony. Perhaps she recalled Judge Drummond berating Robert as he sentenced him. "You should thank God that your venerable father is no more, and that he does not survive to be shocked with the knowledge of your crime...."

At least, Father, you are not alive to know what Robert has done to me this time.

Daisy was five years old at the time of her mother's death. Who she was farmed out to for the next dozen years is anybody's guess. Margaret's other sister, Annie Galbraith, who might have cared for the child, died at the age of twenty-one, when Daisy was six. Robert, her disaster of a father, still clerking in New York, shifted addresses from one year to the next. In February 1881, his wife Lily/Lydia gave birth to Robert's third daughter, variously listed as Jeannette and Janet Notman. (Robert's mother obviously continued to exert a strong hold over him.) Exactly a year later, Robert himself was dead at forty-four.

What are we to make of him? Erstwhile photographer, businessman, convict, clerk, son, brother, charmer, failed husband and father – I could cast him as a backstabbing villain quite easily. It goes without saying that he was flawed and weak, but did he deliberately set out to do harm? If he wanted to make amends with Margaret, set things right after the debacle of the abortion, he showed himself utterly incapable of sustaining his good intentions. If he was not calculatedly cruel, he was most certainly impulsive, insensitive, and irresponsible. In his later photographs, he is dressed like a dandy and looks like a fop. As a human being, he was a flop.

Upon his death, Lily/Lydia either washed her hands of him, or passively allowed the Notman family to take charge. They arranged for Robert's body to be transported back to Montreal, where he was laid to rest next to Annie Birks, the only one of his three wives the family chose to recognize. To this day they lie together beneath an obelisk of pink marble a short distance from the main Notman monument in one of the older sections of Mount Royal Cemetery.

Epilogue

A THICK SHROUD OF SILENCE envelops the Notman family's reaction to Robert's scandalous life. This is hardly surprising given the nature of William's business, so dependent on good repute and public image. Who, after all, would not pause before patronizing – allowing oneself to be touched and handled in the glass room – by the brother of a libertine and scoundrel? At the time of the scandal, Notman was indeed "the well-known photographer," but not so well known that clarification in the press was unnecessary as to which Notman was the accused offender.

Nothing suggests that he ever attended the trial.

Notman's stance was to act as if it all had nothing to do with him. He held his head high and continued to go about his business. At the time of Robert's arrest and incarceration in the Pied-du-Courant Common Gaol, he was advertising in the *Herald* his newly patented artificial skating rink.

NOTMAN'S ARTIFICIAL RINK
Is Now Ready,
And arrangements completed for the various
Styles of
WINTER PHOTOGRAPHY,
Skating, Curling, Snow-Shoeing , &c.
INVENTOR and PATENTEE for this class of portraits,
W. NOTMAN....

Notman's invention consisted of laying a sheet of zinc on the floor, and heaping clumps of rock salt and white fox fur on the surface. Zinc was permeable to the cuts made by skate blades and its reflection in a black and white photograph was a close facsimile to ice. The salt and the fur simulated snow. Customers were invited to bring along their sports equipment for the staged setting, and they did so in droves, Robert's notoriety notwithstanding.

Robert's troubles and the shame he was bringing to the Notman name were only the tip of an iceberg of a year of family sorrow. The death of eleven-year-old Fanny in June 1867, the family's firstborn, froze the hearts of her parents. Six months later William's father died, and his mother was at such a low ebb that there were fears for her life as well. Though no one could replace Fanny, a grieving Alice and William placed hope for the future in the blessing of another pregnancy. Alice began to have confirmation of this hope just as Robert's scandal hit the papers: little George Notman was born in October 1868. Alice read the gory details of Margaret's *accouchement* around the time she began to feel her own baby move. It could not but have caused her to push the reports aside with revulsion.

And yet it would be wrong to think that William Notman abandoned his brother. He posted a quarter of the bail for him, pulled the strings that led to his conditional freedom, and then set him up with a job in Halifax. By the time Charles, William and Alice's last child, was born in December 1870, Robert's affairs seemed completely resolved.

That The Notman Case did no lasting damage to William Notman's reputation is borne out by the persistence of royal patronage. Prince Arthur, the Queen's fourth son – the same young man who disappointed Warden Ferres by failing to show up as scheduled at the penitentiary – was stationed in Canada between 1869 and 1870 in officer training. He came to the studio repeatedly over the course of that period, to be portrayed in all manner of poses and settings, from full royal regalia, to masquerade costume, to "skating" on zinc.

Notman's business expanded and thrived. Over the decades his chain of studios spread across North America and hundreds of thousands of pictures were taken by the dozens of photographers who worked for him. He continued to reap medals at international photography exhibitions for pushing the boundaries of his craft. Over the years, the firm came to include his three sons, and father and sons documented the new Dominion's cities and countryside, its citizens at work and play, the progress of the railroad and the opening of the magnificent new West. Notman's body of work is a visual chronicle of an expansive and dynamic half century, a time when people believed in progress, looked outward, and had faith in the continued forward momentum of life. An astonishing 400,000 prints and negatives still survive at the McCord Museum.

Death came out of the blue for William Notman. He was a vigorous sixty-five-year-old, still actively involved in his business in the fall of 1891 when he caught a bad cold. On November 19, he wrote an upbeat note to his son Charles, then working at the Boston studio, saying that his symptoms were proving to be difficult to dislodge, "and my Dr insists I keep to the house a few days. I do not think there is anything serious – but I go on the principle of being careful." He died of pneumonia six days later.

Despite the odds against it, Daisy Notman made something of herself. After working for several years as a domestic in the home of Vincent and Margaret Hollis or Holsie, an apparently childless carpenter and his wife in their sixties, she was adopted by them. Vincent was American and his wife Scottish and they lived in the Eastern Township district of Brome, where by 1901 they had bought a farm. By her late twenties Daisy was an accomplished seamstress, and in that role inadvertently crossed paths with the as-yet-unborn Marion Louise Phelps, later to be known the length and breadth of the Townships as "Miss Phelps."

Born in 1908 in South Stukely, Miss Phelps lived to a remarkable hundred and five. After decades as a schoolteacher, she devoted herself to local history, and was the prime source for those tracing relatives and ancestors in the region. When in the 1970s, Rosina Fontein, a dogged and redoubtable researcher at the McCord Museum, came calling on Miss Phelps, she was told that Daisy had sewen the bridal dress of Miss Phelps's mother. Also that Notmans closely related to the famous photographer had once lived in the region of South Stukely, but that these Notman relatives were born "on the wrong side of the blanket."

Little wonder that Daisy wanted to put distance between herself and these rumours. According to Miss Phelps, she and a girlfriend moved to New Hartford, Connecticut. She eventually ended up in New York City. She had after all been born there, and was an American citizen. She remained single, became a registered nurse, and enjoyed travel, spending months at a stretch in England and France.

Her passport picture shows a plain, blunt-featured face beneath a cloche hat from which hangs a dotted veil – not an easy photograph to read for clues as to character. I see in the eyes, however, a glint of humour, and on the thin lips a hint of a smile. According to the passport application, she stood five feet five and a half inches tall, had a fair complexion, a large nose, brown hair shot with grey, and – the famous Notman trait – a high forehead. She came into the world with the cards heavily stacked against her, and yet managed to play out a successful game. She died in New York City in 1945.

Less is known about Robert Notman's other daughter, Annie, but she too appears to have led a life of some interest. In 1882 at the age of eighteen she was a member of the staff at the Notman Studio in Montreal, though the general wisdom is that Notman did not use women as photographers. There is a picture of her in that year, the one in which her father died. She cuts an elegant figure, svelte in mourning black, the long sleeves of her gown pulled back to reveal slender wrists and beautifully tapered fingers holding a fan. Hers is not a happy face but one that challenges the camera with a quasi-sullen gaze, as if she can see through all its tricks. By 1888 she had moved on to Boston and was working at a Notman studio there with a fashionable address on Park Street. She later married George Converse, a Boston photographer; they had no children. Like her half-sister Daisy, she lived into her seventies.

Acknowledgements

I GRATEFULLY ACKNOWLEDGE a generous grant from the Canada Council for the Arts that facilitated the research and writing of this book.

Many people helped to orient me in the ways and mores of nineteenth-century Canada and Scotland. Useful tips came my way from Louise Abbott, Mark Abley, Constance Backhouse, Donald Fyson, David Gawley, Michael Leduc, Jane Lewis, Linda Leith, Monique Polak, and Merilyn Simonds. John Kalbfleisch responded to frequent queries about Montreal history with unstinting generosity. Bryan Demchinsky read an early version of the manuscript and provided his customary pithy insights. I thank him for his gift of the book's title.

Thank you to Arlene Royea of the Brome County Historical Society, to Gary Schroder of the Quebec Family History Society, to Youko Leclerc-Desjardins and Cameron Willis of Canada's Penitentiary Museum, to Jo-Ann Savage of the village of South Stukely, and most especially to Paul and Mabel Lindsay of Ardoch Cottage, Gartocharn, Scotland, who went out of their way to introduce me to historic Kilmaronock Church.

Among librarians and archivists, I am as always grateful to the outstanding reference staff of the Eleanor London Côte Saint-Luc Public Library, as well as to Judith Smith of Library and Archives Canada, Christopher Lyons of McGill University's Osler Library of the History of Medicine, and to the ever patient and obliging Michelle of the McLennan Library's microfilm room.

The McCord Museum of McGill University was a gem of a resource for its treasure house of Notman photographs, papers, and memorabilia. Its staff were jewels in their own right. Thank you to Hélène Samson and Heather McNabb for their ever cheerful willingness to share their expertise. I am especially grateful to Heather for unearthing – late in the day – a suppressed secret file in the Notman Papers. The information in it had been compiled by Mrs. Rosina Fontein, a long-retired McCord researcher, whom I never met but in whose footsteps I walked in the last stages of my research.

It is safe to say that this book could not have been written without the guiding hand of Nora Hague. Nora's vast knowledge of and enthusiasm for all things Notman, her compendious storehouse of information about nineteenth-century Montreal, and above all her wholehearted readiness to track down the answer to even the most obscure question, gave me the encouragement to continue sleuthing even when the outlook appeared unpromising.

My agent, Daphne Hart of the Helen Heller Agency, deserves a special mention for her unflagging faith in this book. Many thanks to Nancy Marrelli and Simon Dardick for including this title in their 40th anniversary season. As always, Simon has been an astute and kindly editor.

Finally, the most heartfelt thanks go to my husband Archie Fineberg for his loving reassurance that I would, indeed, be able to pull it off.

Bibliographic Essay

ANYONE WRITING about nineteenth-century Montreal is beholden to the work of Edgar Andrew Collard, and I am in particular grateful for the many rich details to be found in his *Call Back Yesterdays* and *Montreal Yesterdays*. Kathleen Jenkins's *Montreal: Island City of the St. Lawrence* also served as a valuable reference. For the life and career of William Notman, Stanley G. Triggs's books were basic secondary sources, supplemented by my own archival research in the Notman Papers of the McCord Museum. My work was made immeasurably simpler by the *Dictionary of Canadian Biography Online*, which I consulted for biographical information on many of the players. My main sources for the coverage of the Notman case were the city's three most popular daily English papers, the *Gazette*, the *Herald*, and the *Daily Witness*. The digitized version of Lovell's city directory was an invaluable resource for addresses, occupations, and small particulars.

The guiding hand of Nora Hague steered me throughout this project as did its precursor, my CBC *Ideas* documentary "William Notman of Montreal."

CHAPTER 1

For details on mid-century Montreal, see *Call Back Yesterdays*, by Edgar Andrew Collard.

CHAPTER 2

About the life of Dr. Robert Palmer Howard, see article in *Dictionary of Canadian Biography* by Edward Horton Bensley. Information about Dr. Robert Craik comes from his obituary in the *British Medical Journal*, August 18, 1906, 396. Additional information about the "medical gentlemen" was drawn from Joseph Hanaway and Richard Cruess. William Osler's disparaging comment about Dr. Craik is quoted in the June 1997 issue of the *Osler Library Newsletter*.

CHAPTER 3

Information about the early history of the Montreal police force comes from Kathleen Jenkins, 317. For biographical information on Chief Penton, see Collard, *Montreal Yesterdays*, 154, and *Call*

Back Yesterdays, 154-156. The connection between Miss Galbraith and the McGill Normal School was found in a note in the *Gazette*, March 4, 1868. The observation about the well-known photographer not being the Notman implicated in the abortion case was made in the *Gazette*, March 17, 1868.

CHAPTER 4

For details of the early life of William Notman including the bankruptcy, see Triggs, *William Notman: The Stamp of a Studio*. The anecdote about William Senior's love of learning is taken from the recollections of William McFarlane Notman, in the Notman Papers. The childhood reminiscences of William Notman come from the draft of a talk he called "Ruminating" that he gave at a private club in Montreal and that is to be found in the Notman Papers. For the story of Notman at first taking up photography as a hobby, see his lengthy obituary in the *Montreal Witness*, November 26, 1891. On Charles Notman's version of his father's arrival in Montreal, see the essay by him in the Notman Papers. Information about William Senior's imprisonment is derived from an interview with Nora Hague; likewise the detail about letters awaiting the Notman brothers at the Montreal Post Office. The sister's grudge is documented in a letter of Alice Notman, December 28, 1856, in the Notman Papers. Information about Montreal in the 1850s comes from interviews with historian John Kalbfleisch, and from Jenkins, 320. The quotations about Montreal's advantages at mid-century are taken from Ellen James, 2.

CHAPTER 5

Alice Notman's Christmas letter of December 28, 1856 and short memoir of 1878, "Early Days in Canada," are to be found in the Notman Papers, as is William Woodwark's letter.

CHAPTER 6

The description of the wet-plate photography process comes from the endnotes of J. Russell Harper and Stanley Triggs's *Portrait of A Period*, as does the anecdote of the stuffed lamb. The quote about "ten of the largest sized plates yet taken in Canada" is from Triggs, *The Stamp of a Studio*, 24. The source for descriptions of the studio is Triggs, *William Notman's Studio*, 47-51. The long passage about the appearance of the reception room in 1864 comes from *Montreal Business Sketches*, as quoted by Triggs in *William Notman's Studio*, 49. The statistics on female employees were supplied by Nora Hague in an interview, as was the Peeping Tom story. Information on studio backdrops was given by Hélène Samson of the McCord Museum in an interview. The bare-bosom anecdote comes from interview notes made by Triggs in conversation with Charles Notman's son, Geoffrey Notman, October 11, 1968 in the Notman Papers. The religious feelings of William Notman were expressed by him in his letters of March 3, 1861, and January 4, 1864, both in the Notman Papers. The details of the Montreal stay of the Jefferson Davis family are taken from Collard's *Montreal Yesterdays*, 178-180. Collard quotes from Mrs. Lovell's privately printed memoir, *Reminiscences of Seventy Years*.

CHAPTER 7

The reference to Dr. Wilkes and Robert's church attendance is from William Notman's letter of February 22, 1857 in the Notman Papers. On Robert's industriousness, see Alice Notman's letter of April 19, 1857 in the Notman Papers. The details of Robert's physical appearance come from the Prisoners' Record Book of the Kingston Penitentiary, 1843-1890. The apocryphal legend relating to the birth of little Annie was recounted to me by Nora Hague in an interview. The details of the Watts arson case are taken from the *Gazette*, April 18 and 19, 1865.

CHAPTER 8

The German tourist was Johann Georg Koln; the quotation is from the entry on John Ostell by Ellen James in the *Dictionary of Canadian Biography*. The *Gazette* of April 21, 1868 gives the names of the jury as Patrick Curley, William Hart, James Delany, William Crow, Michael Delaney, William Hannan, Alfred Cooper, Charles Higgins, William Murphy, Calixte Berthiaume, Guillaume Chouinard, and X. H. Leclair. Biographical information about Judge Drummond comes from the entry on him in J. Douglas Borthwick, *Montreal Historical Gazeteer*, and in the *Dictionary of Canadian Biography*, by J. I. Little. Borthwick also provides material on Francis Johnson, whose life is sketched by Clinton O. White in the *Dictionary of Canadian Biography*. The accounts of the Patterson trial are taken from the *Gazette*, June 26 and June 27, 1861, and from the Montreal *Pilot*, June 29, 1861. The quotation from Johnson about the lost force of the evidence in translation is from the *Pilot*. On Judge Aylwin, see the *Dictionary of Canadian Biography* entry by André Garon. The insight into the sympathies of Victorian judges and juries comes from Constance Blackhouse, *Petticoats & Prejudice*, 50. The details of the expected execution are derived from the *Gazette*, September 7, 1861, and from a column entitled "One Hanging Wasn't Enough" by John Kalbfleisch in the *Gazette*, September 7, 2009. The letter to the editor questioning Patterson's sentence is from the *Gazette*, July 26, 1861.

CHAPTER 9

The editorial in the *British American Journal* was reprinted in the *Gazette*, July 26, 1861. The quote about a child a year is from Wendy Mitchinson, 134, footnote 36. For the early history of abortion, see *Wikipedia*, "Abortion." On the subject of abortion being treated as a private concern in Britain and its colonies until the nineteenth century, see Constance Backhouse, "Involuntary Motherhood," 61. This article is also the source for background on the law of 1803, for quotes about mother love, and for Queen Victoria's letter, 62-65. Backhouse quotes McLaren ("They took pills not to abort, but to 'bring on their period.'"), 69. On the subject of jurors' leniency towards infanticide, see Backhouse, "Involuntary Motherhood," 65. On the general attitude of leniency towards perpetrators of infanticide, see Backhouse, *Petticoats & Prejudice*, 163. The advertisement for Holloway's pills ran in the *Gazette*, April 4, 1861, and is quoted in Peter Gossage, 6. The description of the contents of patent medicines is from Gossage, 4. The figures on American abortions are from Olasky, 57. On the ideas of Edwin M. Hale, see Olasky, 152. On Madame Restell's arrest, Olasky, 160. On spiritism and abortion, Olasky 66-80. On the decline of the middle-class birth rate and anxiety around the fertility of the poor, see Backhouse, "Involuntary Motherhood," 80.

CHAPTER 10

The quote about the Galbraiths and losing causes is from George Eyre-Todd's romantic history of the Loch Lomond area, 46-47. The quote about the timelessness of Kilmaronock comes from the privately printed pamphlet *Loch Lomond Village* by Joan Pearson. On the mobility of rural Scots, see T.M. Devine, 482-483. Information about the life of Alexander Tilloch Galt is from the entry about him in the *Dictionary of Canadian Biography* by Jean-Pierre Kesteman. On the early history of South Stukely, see Mrs. C. M. Day, 356-361. On the culture of Scottish Presbyterianism in Canada, see W. Stanford Reid, 5; 128-131. For biographical information on William Dawson, see the entry on him in the *Dictionary of Canadian Biography* by Peter R. Eakins and Jean Sinnamon Eakins. On the inauguration ceremonies of the Normal School, see E.A. Paradissis, 4. The "Special Regulations for Government and Discipline" are taken from the "Principal's Memoranda of Minutes & Regulations of the McGill Normal School," in the McGill University Archives. The list of professors at the Normal School comes from Paradissis, 41.

CHAPTER 11

The description of the criminal courtroom of the Court House is from Ellen James, 143-154. An abbreviated version of the indictment appeared in the *Daily Witness*, April 21, 1868. On the historic connection between ergot and childbirth, *Wikipedia*, "Ergot." The account of the proceedings of the first day of the trial has been spliced together from reports in the *Gazette*, the *Herald*, and the *Daily Witness*, all of April 21, 1868. Biographical information on T. K. Ramsay is taken from the entry on him by Jean-Charles Bonenfant in the *Dictionary of Canadian Biography*. For Bernard Devlin, likewise see the entry by Jean-Charles Bonenfant in the *Dictionary of Canadian Biography*. Biographical information on William Warren Hastings Kerr is found in Borthwick. Nora Hague alerted me to the story of Letitia Chambers and David McCord and supplied me with anecdotal information about them in an interview. See also the entry on David McCord in the *Dictionary of Canadian Biography* by Pamela Miller. On the rigidity of the thinking of MacVicar and Dawson at a time of relative relaxation of fundamentalist views, see

Reid, 128. The connection between Devlin and Drummond over a former abortion case is traced by Michael McCulloch, 49-66.

CHAPTER 12

Dr. Irvine's sermon ran in the *Daily Witness*, March 10, 1868. About the shipwrecks of the *Anglo Saxon*, see Frank Galgay and Michael McCarthy. The quote from the *Glasgow Times* is from its issue of June 24, 1868. For biographical information about Dr. Girdwood, see Hanaway and Cruess, 54, as well as the entry on him in the *Dictionary of Canadian Biography* by Denis Goulet. On creating firelight with a magnesium flare, see Triggs, *Stamp of a Studio*, 26 and Hanaway and Cruess, 168.

CHAPTER 13

The account of the proceedings of the second day of the trial has been spliced together from reports in the *Gazette*, the *Herald*, the *Daily Witness*, and the *Quebec Morning Chronicle*, all of April 22, 1868. For information about Hugh McLennan, see the entry on him by Allan Levine in the *Dictionary of Canadian Biography*. On the pedigree of Sir William Fenwick, see John Kalbfleisch, 68. On the story of Henry Hogan and the St. Lawrence Hall, see Collard, *Montreal Yesterdays*, 132-150.

CHAPTER 14

For biographical information on Dr. Duncan Campbell MacCallum, see Hanaway and Cruess, 163.

CHAPTER 15

For the judge's charge, see *Daily Witness*, April 22, 1868 and the *Gazette* and the *Herald* April 23, 1868. For events of the remainder of the trial, see the *Daily Witness*, *Gazette*, and *Herald*, April 24 to April 30, 1868. For biographical information about Dr. George Fenwick, see Hanaway and Cruess, 60-63.

CHAPTER 16

Much of the material in this chapter is based on my original research in the Kingston Penitentiary Prisoners Record Books, Prisoners

Liberation Books, and Warden's Journals and Correspondence available on microfilm from Library and Archives Canada. I am grateful to Cameron Willis of the Kingston Penitentiary Museum for supplying detailed information about prison life by means of e-mail exchanges, which are listed below.

Information about the transport of prisoners from the railway station to Kingston Penitentiary came from Cameron Willis, March 6, 2013. The quote that begins "a school of reform...." is from the *Kingston Chronicle & Gazette*, 6 September 1834, quoted by Jennifer McKendry, 165. For the history of Kingston Penitentiary, see Jennifer McKendry, J.A. Edmison, and the Corrections Canada website. See also *Rules and Regulations* [of Kingston Penitentiary] by Wolfred Nelson and Andrew Dickson. Biographical information on MacDonell comes from the entry on him in the *Dictionary of Canadian Biography* by J. K. Johnson; on William Coverdale, the entry by Margaret S. Angus. For the history of Eldon Hall, see the website of the Portsmouth Community Correctional Centre. On the reception process at Kingston Penitentiary, see Oswald C.J. Withrow, 5-6. The detailed description of prison uniforms is from Cameron Willis, March 6, 2013. For the long quote beginning "Avenues of inspection..." see McKendry, 168. For the description of cells, see McKendry, 165-167. "Confinement on Sunday [is the worst punishment,]" said Thomas Emond, at the time of his liberation, October 1, 1869. Information about the letter-writing process came from Cameron Willis, March 20, 2013. Robert Notman's letter to his mother is to be found in the Convicts Letter Register, Book 10, 168. "Mr. Bell was a very disagreeable..." John Paxton, at the time of his liberation, 6 August 1869. Biographical information on Ferres comes from the entry on him in the *Dictionary of Canadian Biography* by Lorne Ste. Croix. Creighton's assessment of Ferres is to be found in this article. For the description of the Dark Cell, see McKendry, 167. Information on Narcisse Bernard comes from the Liberation Book entry on him for November 13, 1866, and the Prisoner's Record Register for February 1867. Cameron Willis supplied the details of Bernard's escape from Rockwood Asylum in an e-mail April 10, 2013. The statistics on mental illness come from the Corrections Canada website. On Reverend Mulkins's habits, see James Jack, Liberation Book, July 31, 1869.

CHAPTER 17

Judge Monk's ruling was reported in the *Daily Witness*, April 7, 1869. Devlin's sarcastic comment ["It would be strange if this court …"] is from the *Gazette*, October 5, 1869. On the details of life within the Montreal common jail, see Alexandre-Maurice Delisle. The fact that repairs were being made to the heating system of the courthouse was reported in the *Gazette*, October 22, 1869. The estimate as to bail in today's dollars was made based on information on the website davemanuel.com/inflation. Biographical information on Dr. Godfrey comes from the *New York Medical Journal*, 21, 661. Backhouse writes of the campaign against seducers in Toronto in *Petticoats & Prejudice*, 237.

CHAPTER 18

The tale of men bribing their way out of Kingston Penitentiary comes from Oswald Withrow, 2. The information about Robert managing the new branch in Halifax came by way of an interview with Nora Hague, as did the information about the circumstances of Sir John A. Macdonald's photograph in 1869. Sir John A.'s private letter is from the Macdonald Papers, as referenced by Backhouse, *Petticoats & Prejudice*, 166.

CHAPTER 19

The genealogist in question – on the recommendation of Nora Hague – was Gary Schroder. "I suspect that if there was a marriage…" Schroder's e-mail to me, September 23, 2012. On the history of Stanstead, see Matthew Farfan, "Stanstead's Heritage at a Glance," *Township Heritage Web Magazine*. The report of the *Stanstead Journal* on the Notman trial is from its issue of April 30, 1868. The baptism record of Margaret Janet (Daisy) Notman comes from an official website of the Church of Jesus Christ of Latter-Day Saints researched for me by Nora Hague. Biographical information on George Converse was supplied to me in an e-mail by Hélène Samson, April 23, 2013.

CHAPTER 20

The summary of William Notman's business history is from Gordon Doods, Roger Hall, and Stantley G. Triggs, *The World of William Notman*, 61.

Selected Bibliography

Backhouse, Constance. "Involuntary Motherhood: Abortion, Birth Control and the Law in Nineteenth Century Canada." *Windsor Yearbook of Access to Justice* 3 (1983): 61-130.

Black [Adam and Charles]. *Black's Picturesque Tourist of Scotland.* 16th ed. Edinburgh: Adam and Charles Black, 1863.

Borthwick, J. Douglas. *Montreal History and Gazetteer to 1892.* Montreal: John Lovell & Son, 1892.

Collard, Edgar Andrew. *Call Back Yesterdays.* Toronto: Longmans, 1965.

Collard, Edgar Andrew. *Montreal Yesterdays.* Toronto: Longmans, 1962.

Day, Mrs. C.M. *History of the Eastern Townships.* Montreal: John Lovell, 1869.

Delisle, Alexandre-Maurice, *General Rules and Regulations for the Interior Order and Police of the Common Gaol of Montreal* [Montreal?], 1864.

Denham, John. "Does Ergot of Rye Act as a Poison on the Child in Utero?" *Dublin Quarterly Journal of Medical Science.* (January 1851): 31-45.

Devine, T.M. *The Scottish Nation, 1700-2007.* London: Penguin 2006.

Dodds, Gordon, Roger Hall, and Stanley G. Triggs. *The World of William Notman.* Boston: David R. Godine, 1993.

Edis, Arthur W. "Tarnier and Denham on Ergot of Rye." *The London Medical Record.* (February 26, 1873): 114-115.

Edmison, J. A. "The History of Kingston Penitentiary." *Transactions of the Kingston Historical Society* (1953-54): 26-35.

Edwards, Reginald. "Theory, History, and Practice of Education: Fin de siècle and a New Beginning." *McGill Journal of Education.* (Fall 1991): 237-266.

Eyre-Todd, George. *Loch Lomond, Loch Katrine and the Trossachs.* Edinburgh: Blackie & Son, c. 1922.

Fenwick, George E., and Francis Wayland Campbell. "The Notman Abortion Case." *Canada Medical Journal and Monthly Record,* 4 (1868), 522-524.

Galgay, Frank, and Michael McCarthy. *Shipwrecks of Newfoundland and Labrador.* St. John's: Harry Cuff, 1981.

Gossage, Peter. "Absorbing Junior: the Use of Patent Medicines as Abortifacients in Nineteenth-Century Montreal." The [McGill] *Register* 1 (March 1982):1-13.

Hanaway, Joseph, and Richard Cruess, *McGill Medicine: The First Half Century, 1829-1885.* Montreal: McGill-Queen's University Press, 1996.

Harper, J. Russell, and Stanley G. Triggs, eds. *Portrait of a Period: A Collection of Notman Photographs, 1856 to 1915.* Montreal: McGill University Press, 1967.

Herman, Arthur. *How the Scots Invented the Modern World.* New York: Three Rivers Press, 2001.

James, Ellen S. "The Civil Architecture of John Ostell." Ph.D. diss., McGill University, 1982.

Jenkins, Kathleen. *Montreal: Island City of the St. Lawrence.* New York: Doubleday, 1966.

Kalbfleisch, John. *This Island in Time: Remarkable Tales from Montreal's Past.* Montreal: Véhicule Press, 2008.

McCulloch, Michael. "Dr. Tumblety, the Indian Herb Doctor: Politics, Professionalism, and Abortion in Mid-Nineteenth-Century Montreal." *Canadian Bulletin of Medical History* 10(1) (1993): 49-66.

McGoogan, Ken. *How the Scots Invented Canada.* Toronto: HarperCollins, 2010.

McKendry, Jennifer. "Controlling Society through Architectural Design." In *With Our Past Before Us: Nineteenth-Century Architecture in the Kingston Area.* Toronto: University of Toronto Press, 1995.

McLaren, Angus, and Arlene Tigar McLaren. *The Bedroom and the State: The Changing Practices and Politics of Contraception and Abortion in Canada, 1880-1997.* 2nd ed. Toronto: Oxford University Press, 1997.

Mitchinson, Wendy. *The Nature of Their Bodies: Women and Their Doctors in Victorian Canada.* Toronto: University of Toronto Press, 1991.

Nuala O'Faolain. *The Story of Chicago May.* New York: Riverhead Books, 2005.

Olasky, Marvin. *Abortion Rites: A Social History of Abortion in America.* Wheaton, IL: Crossway Books, 1992.

Paradissis, E.A. *The McGill Normal School: A Brief History, 1857-1907.* M.A. thesis, McGill University, 1982.

Pearson, Joan. *Loch Lomond Village: Story of Gartocharn and the Parish of Kilmaronock, Dunbartonshire.* Glasgow, 1971.

Phenix, Patricia. *Private Demons: The Tragic Personal Life of Sir John A. Macdonald.* Toronto: McClelland & Stewart, 2006.

Reid, W. Stanford, ed. *The Scottish Tradition in Canada*. Toronto: McClelland & Stewart, 1976.

Wallace, W. Stewart. "Elementary School Education in Canada." *The Encyclopedia of Canada*. 4 (1948): 265-270.

Rose, George Maclean, ed. *Cyclopaedia of Canadian Bigoraphy*. Toronto: Rose Publishing, 1888.

Thompson, Charles M. "Ergot of Rye in Abortion and Hemorrhage," *The Lancet* 12 (303) (1829): 365-366.

Triggs, Stanley. *William Notman: The Stamp of a Studio*. Toronto: Coach House Press, 1986.

Triggs, Stanley. *William Notman's Studio: The Canadian Picture*. Montreal: McCord Museum, 1992.

Withrow, Dr. Oswald C. J. *Shackling the Transgressor: An Indictment of the Canadian Penal System*. Toronto: Thomas Nelson & Sons, 1933.